GANDHI

── on ──

CHRISTIANITY

GANDHI

—— on ——

CHRISTIANITY

Edited by Robert Ellsberg

ORBIS BOOKS

Maryknoll, New York 10545

The Catholic Foreign Mission Society of America (Maryknoll) recruits and trains people for overseas missionary service. Through Orbis Books, Maryknoll aims to foster the international dialogue that is essential to mission. The books published, however, reflect the opinions of their authors and are not meant to represent the official position of the society.

Copyright © 1991 by Orbis Books

Published by Orbis Books, Maryknoll, NY 10545

Writings of Gandhi copyright © Navajivan Trust, by the permission of Navajivan Trust, Ahmedabad-380 0 14 (India).

Selections from Gandhi were compiled from the following sources:

M. K. Gandhi, *Christian Missions: Their Place in India*, edited by Bharatan Kumarappa (Ahmedabad: Navajivan Publishing House, 1941); M. K. Gandhi, "What Jesus Means to Me," compiled by R. K. Prabhu (Ahmedabad: Navajivan Publishing House, 1959); M. K. Gandhi, *The Message of Jesus*, edited by Anand T. Hingorani (Bombay: Bharatiya Vidya Bhavan, 1964); M. K. Gandhi, *In Search of the Supreme*, vol. III, edited by V. B. Kher (Ahmedabad: Navajivan Publishing House, 1962); M. K. Gandhi, *Truth Is God*, edited by R. K. Prabhu (Ahmedabad: Navajivan Publishing House, 1955); M. K. Gandhi, *My Religion*, edited by Bharatan Kumarappa (Ahmedabad: Navajivan Publishing House, 1955).

Information on original sources is indicated after each selection as it appears in the texts cited above. Gandhi's *Autobiography* was first published in book-form in English in 1929. His weekly *Young India* was published from 1919-1931 and *Harijan* from 1933 on.

Library of Congress Cataloging-in-Publication Data

Gandhi, Mahatma, 1869-1948.
    [Selections. 1991]
    Gandhi on Christianity / edited by Robert Ellsberg.
      p. cm.
    Includes bibliographical references.
    1. Christianity. 2. Religions. I. Ellsberg, Robert, 1955-
II. Title.
    BR123.G262   1991
200 — dc20   91-23278
                                        CIP

Contents

Chapter Four   57
All Religions Are True

Part Two
CHRISTIAN RESPONSE

Chapter Five   77
Gandhian Guidelines for a World of Religious Difference
by Diana L. Eck

Introduction

Robert Ellsberg

Mohandas K. Gandhi, hero of the Indian independence movement and one of history's most compelling examples of political sagacity and personal holiness, has always presented a special attraction and challenge for Christians. As a young lawyer in South Africa he was pursued by numerous evangelical friends who avidly sought his conversion. Always open to the truth, from whatever its source, Gandhi gave serious consideration to such appeals, read the Bible, and attended church services and prayer meetings. In the end he was left confirmed in the Hindu faith of his birth. But it was a faith always open to a greater truth, a truth larger, as he perceived it, than the capacity of any person, church, or tradition to contain it completely.

Later, as he came to regard the personal search for truth as inseparable from the public struggle for freedom and justice, Gandhi posed a differen' kind of challenge. Here was a Hindu who politely rejected the dogmatic claims of Christianity while embracing, with every ounce of his will, the ethical claims of Christ. Christians were among his earliest disciples in South Africa. Some, like C. F. Andrews, the English missionary and an early biographer, remained friends and companions for life. Others, like Dietrich Bonhoeffer, Peter Maurin, and Jacques Maritain, studied him from afar.

In either case, Gandhi's influence on Christians has owed little to his specific comments on Jesus or Christianity but rather to his ability to recall, in his witness, the features of Christ and the gospel commandment of love. The past decades have been distinguished by many Christian prophets of nonviolence: Dorothy Day of the Catholic Worker, Danilo Dolci in Sicily, Lanza del Vasto in France, Cesar Chavez, Thomas Merton. All of them traced their vision to the teachings and witness of Jesus. But just as surely they acknowledged that it was by way of Gandhi, and not through the teachings of the Christian churches, that they encountered the nonviolent face of Christ.

Before Gandhi there had always been individuals committed to nonviolence as a personal or religious code. Likewise, history records many instances of successful nonviolent action. But Gandhi was remarkable for his union of theory and practice. He demonstrated that the same spirit of nonviolence he embraced as a principle of life could be harnessed as a principle of effective political struggle.

Of all the Christian interpreters of Gandhi, undoubtedly the most well-known in the West was Martin Luther King, Jr. In his leadership of the black freedom movement in the American South, he struggled to join the inspiration of the gospel with the method and philosophy of Gandhi. Describing his discovery of Gandhi, King wrote,

> As I delved into the philosophy of Gandhi my skepticism concerning the power of love gradually diminished, and I came to see for the first time that the Christian doctrine of love operating through the Gandhian method of nonviolence was one of the most potent weapons available to oppressed people in their struggle for freedom ... This principle became the guiding light of our movement. Christ furnished the spirit and motivation while Gandhi furnished the method.

Gandhi's ethic was not simply a matter of "turning the other cheek." He had discovered what he called "truth-force," a power against which guns, blows, and prison bars were ultimately powerless. Gandhi's word for this was *Satyagraha*, "clinging-to-truth"—derived from the Sanskrit word *sat*, literally, "that which is." He believed that nonviolence offered a means of struggle rooted in the nature of reality itself. For Gandhi was convinced that beneath the apparent conflicts and divisions of life there was an underlying principle of love or truth. Satyagraha was designed to bring that reality to the surface, to act on it, to make it visible, if need be, by hardship or suffering undertaken in a spirit of detachment from results.

The goal of nonviolent struggle was not the victory of one side over another but a radical transformation of relationships. The object was not the conquest of power but of truth. In such a struggle the choice of means could not be left to discretion. The identity between means and ends was an essential axiom of Gandhi's philosophy. Thus, deceit, manipulation, and any kind of violence against persons were utterly incompatible with the goal of truth—the ultimate horizon that lay beyond any immediate objective, whether the redress of a local injustice, or the achievement of Indian self-rule. As he stated in one of his most potent formulas: Truth is God.

The suggestion that Jesus, in his life and teachings espoused a similar nonviolent ethic has remained one of the most well-guarded secrets of Christian history. A concept of truth as the exclusive property of one religion or church has inspired the torture of heretics, the Crusades, and a hundred wars of religion. A distinction between the "counsel of perfection" and the demands of patriotism has allowed Christians to bless and serve on both sides of every war in the history of the West. Gandhi helped restore to the Christian West the "dangerous memory" of the Sermon on the Mount and Jesus' radical commandment of love. For this fact alone Gandhi has earned a place in the history of Christianity. And yet Gandhi's philosophy of nonviolence is not the focus of this book. There remain other dimensions to the dialogue between Gandhi and Christianity, some of which are explored in the pages that follow—both in Gandhi's own words and through the thoughtful reflections of several contemporary Christian writers.

GANDHI AND CHRISTIANITY

Gandhi's writings amply document his profound appreciation of Jesus, the influence of Christian ideals, and his devotion to many Christian friends. His frequent recourse to Christian scripture led spiteful critics to accuse him of being a "secret Christian," a charge Gandhi considered both a libel and a compliment: "a libel because there are men who believe me to be capable of being secretly anything . . . a compliment in that it is a reluctant acknowledgment of my capacity for appreciating the beauties of Christianity." Indeed, if left with the Sermon on the Mount and his own interpretation of it, he said he would gladly call himself a Christian. But he conceded honestly that his interpretation would fall short of orthodoxy.

Gandhi's difficulties with Christianity were at once theological and ethical. He could not bring himself to regard Jesus Christ as the only Son of God. Nor could he accept that his salvation hinged on such a confession. At the same time, the behavior of Christians left him doubtful that their religion had any superior claim to be uniquely true. Not only was the "Christian" West embroiled, in his lifetime, in two world wars, but the monarchs of England and all their agents of empire were church-going worshippers of Christ.

Gandhi's encounters with Christianity, as recounted in his autobiography, began with the disdainful childhood memory that Indian converts were somehow required to renounce their cultural heritage, to embrace "beef and brandy." Later, as a law student in England, he met his first Christians and began his acquaintance with the Bible. It was in South Africa, however, where he lived from 1893 to 1915, that he enjoyed his first extensive contacts with Christians. These were mostly evangelical Protestants who invited him to prayer services and entreated him earnestly to accept Christ as his personal savior. Gandhi appreciated the sincerity and good will behind such efforts; he responded with similar good will in his efforts to understand the Christian faith. In the end, however, his religious quest led him back to the riches of Hinduism.

At the same time, however, his life was permanently enriched by his discovery of a Christian writer, Leo Tolstoy. The Russian novelist, renowned for *Anna Karenina* and *War and Peace*, had devoted himself, in his later years, to explicating what he called the true message of Jesus, as represented in the Sermon on the Mount. The essential message was to be found in "the law of love," the absolute rejection of violence in all its forms.

Tolstoy's Christian pacifism was joined with a reverence for the poor, a philosophy of "bread labor," and a commitment to simplicity of life—ideals only imperfectly realized in his own life, but which found an immediate resonance in the Indian lawyer. Gandhi's understanding of nonviolence was ultimately more sophisticated, but among other things, Gandhi found in Tolstoy confirmation of his own inclination to distinguish freely between the message of Jesus and the teachings and practice of the Christian church. Thus, Jesus remained for Gandhi an object of reverence and devotion, uncompromised by the failures and betrayals of his Christian followers.

By the time he returned to India Gandhi had developed the essential features of his philosophy of nonviolence. For the next forty years, until his death in 1948, he tried to perfect this philosophy in action. Largely through the force of his extraordinary personality and the purity of his example, he helped his people make the psychological transition from servitude to freedom.

History celebrates such famous campaigns as the March to the Sea, when Gandhi courted arrest by defying the British monopoly on the production and sale of salt. But time spent on such dramatic gestures was relatively little compared with the equally important, if far less obviously revolutionary activity of sitting at his spinning wheel, producing homespun cloth. Only free men and women could win freedom for India. It was really this change of consciousness, grounded at the level of the common villager, and not simply the public campaigns of civil disobedience, that made the achievement of independence inevitable. Still, this achievement paled beside his ultimate, and ultimately elusive, goal—the Kingdom of God.

As deeply as he came to identify with the soul of India, Gandhi maintained his extensive contact and dialogue with a wide assortment of Christians. The population of native Christians in India was then, as it remains, quite small. According to a 1921 census they represented only one and a half percent of the population, concentrated mostly in the south. Thus, Gandhi's encounters with Christians were largely with foreigners, many of them missionaries who sought interviews regarding his opinion of Jesus, Christianity, and the missionary enterprise in general.

On these various subjects Gandhi expressed himself in definite terms. He confessed his sincere devotion to the figure of Jesus, whom he regarded as an ideal representative of Satyagraha. He embraced not only the Sermon on the Mount but Jesus' redemptive suffering unto death, and his example of loving service as the essence of true religion. At the same time he voiced his criticism of orthodox Christianity, both for its dogmatic claims and its ethical contributions. Christendom, judging from his experience on the receiving end, appeared to represent the very negation of the Sermon on the Mount. On the subject of Christian missionary activity in India he was particularly outspoken. He believed that most missionaries harbored disdain for the traditions and culture of India and were blind to their own identification of the gospel with Western civilization. He rejected the teaching that salvation was available only through Christianity and regarded the pursuit of converts as a form of spiritual imperialism that violated his own belief in the equality of all faiths. As for proselytizing, he believed that any authentic witness to one's faith should be offered in deeds, rather than words. When faith was lived it was self-propagating.

Gandhi had a similar attitude toward other faiths—particularly Buddhism and Islam: appreciation for all that he identified with the common deposit of truth; criticism for all expressions of intolerance and fanaticism. He believed that all religions were essentially true—all of them paths to the same Truth. Likewise, all were imperfect, liable to error, and in need of purification. The same was true of Hinduism. He was tireless in his condemnation of those Hindu practices, such as the oppression of Untouchables, that he regarded as blasphemous perversions of religious truth. It is quite possible that he devoted even more of his time to the cause of the Untouchables—the Children of God, as he called them—and to the cause of religious tolerance than he did to the direct struggle against the British Empire. Indeed, he could not have distinguished one cause from another. In any case, it was ultimately his commitment to reconciliation between warring creeds that cost him his life. Shortly after Independence and the bloody partition of India and Pakistan—a schism he did everything in his power to prevent—he was murdered by Hindu extremists who felt betrayed by his concern for the welfare of Muslims.

This fact serves as a reminder that Gandhi's writings on the world religions—including Christianity—were not conceived in academic isolation, nor in the friendly exchange of an ecumenical parliament, but in the midst of intense social and political strife. The British rulers derived an advantage from the divisions between Hindus, Muslims, and Untouchables. Thus, Gandhi's views on Christianity and other religions had a direct bearing on the struggle for independence. But Gandhi's efforts to overcome interreligious or communal rivalries were rooted in a much deeper struggle, the creation of a nonviolent society beyond Independence.

The communal bloodletting that accompanied the British transfer of power offered compelling testimony to the imperative of religious tolerance and interreligious dialogue. But Gandhi's belief in the equality of all religions was not based primarily on pragmatic reasoning. It went to the heart of his understanding of Truth, a reality larger than any one religion, but in which all were ultimately grounded. As surely in the dialogue with other faiths as in the struggle against injustice, nonviolence was the way to Truth. It was a way, furthermore, that must lead one into the midst of conflict. For Gandhi, who more than anyone of his age or since defined a new kind of political holiness, God was not to be found in a Himalayan cave, but precisely in the identification with the poorest of the poor, and in their struggle for dignity and well-being.

GANDHI'S CHALLENGE

The critical commentaries included in this volume treat at least four types of challenge which Gandhi poses to contemporary Christians.

CHALLENGE TO INTERRELIGIOUS DIALOGUE

Since Gandhi's time there have been enormous advances in dialogue between Christians and people of other faiths. In ecumenical and academic circles it is widely accepted that the nature of dialogue requires mutual respect, a degree of humility, and a recognition that no party has an exclusive monopoly on the truth. Recently there have been signs that the challenge of dialogue is entering a new phase. At one time the principal motive of dialogue, at least from a Christian perspective, was to convert the "non-believer." Later this gave way to a respectful effort to hear and understand the faith of others—perhaps even to reach an appreciation, in Christian terms, of the truth or salvific meaning of the other's faith. A new function of dialogue is achieved when, among the other fruits of interreligious encounter, each side is open to the possibility of a new self-understanding. In other words, it is one thing to acknowledge that a Hindu may achieve salvation. One may furthermore attempt to understand how this is possible through the universal saving will of God as revealed in Christ. At this point, however, one might go farther still and ask how one's own understanding of Christ may be enlarged or modified on the basis of the encounter with Hinduism. Is it possible to understand salvation through Christ in Hindu or Buddhist terms?

Gandhi has much to offer Christians engaged in this enterprise, not least for his contribution of what Diana Eck terms "Gandhian principles of interreligious dialogue." It is also extremely important in the project of dialogue that Christians begin to see how they are perceived by others. Even Christians who have achieved some sophistication in their interpretation of other faiths may have little experience in seeing themselves through others' eyes. Gandhi's relatively sympathetic assessment of Christianity makes his friendly criticism all the more significant and telling.

Not all those engaged in interreligious dialogue are prepared to accept Gandhi's belief in the equality of all religions. Many more would share an interest in the concern to affirm the uniqueness of their own faith without falling prey to idolatry, fanaticism, or lack of charity. But Gandhi steers the conversation to an even greater challenge: the hope that all the various forms of religious faith on this planet may learn to confront in cooperation the global threats to our common survival. Interreligious understanding need not and indeed must not be separated from issues of human liberation, peace, and the good of the earth.

THE CHALLENGE TO ASIAN THEOLOGY

Gandhi was one of the first to insist on the distinction between the gospel of Christ and Western culture and civilization. Jesus, he claimed, was himself an Asiatic whose teachings were distorted by their encounter with the power of Rome. If Christianity had a universal message, why must it be presented in Western language, in terms of Western history, and from a Western point of view?

These questions have emerged as a strong challenge for Asian Christian theologians. If Christianity is to be a viable force in Asia, they argue, it is not enough that it be clothed superficially in Asian garb. It must become thoroughly incarnate or inculturated in Asian traditions, philosophy, and habits of thought. Such convictions are now widely shared in Asia. Indian theologians, particularly the Jesuits (of whom Ignatius Jesudasan is representative), have looked to Gandhi as a special partner in dialogue.

Gandhi's genius, as a leader of the independence movement, was to recognize that Indians could not effectively oppose British colonialism while adopting the trappings of English culture. When Gandhi appeared for tea with the King of England, his dress — a homespun loincloth — made a statement far more eloquent than a hundred manifestos. (When asked whether he hadn't felt underdressed for the occasion, he replied that the King had worn clothes enough for the two of them.)

Asian Christians face the challenge to seek their own particular identity in the midst of the masses who are mostly non-Christian and mostly poor. Consequently, many have argued that the road to an authentically Asian Christianity leads in a special way to inculturation, to interreligious dialogue, and to solidarity with the oppressed. In all these tasks, Gandhi represents an indispensable guide.

THE CHALLENGE TO CHRISTIAN DISCIPLESHIP

I have already alluded to the influence of Gandhi on the development of Christian nonviolence. Jim Douglass, a Christian veteran of many Gandhian campaigns, shows in his essay how Gandhi may help Christians recover the full and radical meaning of the cross. All too often the cross has been reduced to pietistic or individualistic terms. Gandhi rejected a spirituality focused on personal salvation; the quest for personal enlightenment was inseparable from the life of service and the commitment to social transformation. In the terms of liberation theology, Gandhi urged Christians to express *orthodoxy* in terms of *orthopraxis*. Jesus, as Gandhi observed, called human beings not to a new religion but to a new life. Gandhi's experiments in nonviolence challenge Christians to see the suffering figure of Christ through new eyes.

With good humor, Gandhi resisted those Christians who held the opinion that "if only he accepted Christ" his example would be perfect. By the same token, he never sought to convert others to his own Hindu faith. His hope, always, was that his example would help Muslims to become better Muslims, and Christians to become better Christians. There are many Christians who have become better Christians because of Gandhi, who have rediscovered different emphases in the gospel, who have been reminded of Jesus' words: "It is not all those who say 'Lord, Lord,' who will enter into the Kingdom of Heaven ... "

THE CHALLENGE TO CHRISTIAN MISSION

The Western Christian missionary enterprise has always faced the criticism that it followed the path of colonial power and trade. Even when courageous missionaries defended native peoples, there was no escaping the fact that they represented the religion of the conquerors. Western missionaries were often oblivious of their tendency to confuse the gospel with the benefits of Western culture, progress, and technical know-how; with the best of intentions, they could easily become agents of cultural alienation. Thus, even while building schools and hospitals, many missionaries failed to see how their relative wealth and prosperity fostered feelings of dependence and resentment. Many natives were induced—whether consciously or not—to convert to Christianity as a path of upward mobility. On the most vital theological level, furthermore, the great missionary endeavors were often built on the questionable premise that non-Christians were heathens whose only route to salvation lay in their incorporation into the Christian fold. Gandhi was acutely sensitive to all these concerns—so much so that the best thing he could say about foreign missionaries in India was that they had unintentionally inspired many Indians to renew their own Hindu or Muslim faith.

Since Gandhi's time, such criticisms have been felt and taken to heart by many Western missionary organizations—both Protestant and Catholic. Less frequently is mission identified with baptizing "pagan babies"; increasingly it is identified with the life of the church in the world, an "integral evangelization" that addresses the many levels of human existence. The mission of Jesus was not to proclaim a religion called "Christianity," but the Kingdom of God drawn near. The church that lives by his name shares in that mission.

Thus, there is no question that the church's mission requires involvement in the promotion of peace, justice, and the values of the Kingdom. However, as these values are not the exclusive property of Christians, the church seeks cooperation with other religions and all people of good will. Furthermore, the Catholic church, at least since Vatican II, and many Protestants as well, have publicly acknowledged that God wills the salvation of all people and that such salvation is available in all religious faiths. Gandhi himself may have helped promote this theological insight. Many Christians could easily have adopted Gandhi's own statement, with him in mind: "If I have read the Bible correctly, I know many men who have never heard the name of Jesus Christ or have even rejected the official interpretation of Christianity who will, probably, if Jesus came in our midst today in the flesh, be owned by him more than many of us."

Of course this has raised serious questions about the rationale and methods of foreign missionary activity, particularly in predominantly non-Christian lands. These questions do not efface the missionary impulse that is essential to the logic and life of Christianity. But they have prompted deep soul-searching, rethinking, and a process of self-emptying—of wealth, of power, of privilege, as well as triumphalism, arrogance, and feelings of superiority. Only when this is accomplished can the gospel shine forth in its unadorned purity.

Bob McCahill, the Maryknoll priest who has contributed to this volume, would appear to satisfy Gandhi's image of the ideal missionary. In his work in the villages of Bangladesh he has endeavored to allow the fragrance of the gospel to emanate from his service and dialogue of life among his Muslim neighbors. He demonstrates yet another way in which the Sermon on the Mount may be lived in Gandhian terms. In fact, he deserves credit and thanks here for originally suggesting this book.

The purpose of this volume is not to "claim" Gandhi for Christianity, nor to subject his views on Christianity to theological critique. Rather, the intention is to extend and deepen the conversation between Gandhi and Christians with the hope that Christian readers, in particular, might respond to Gandhi's challenge with new self-understanding and renewed faith. Increasingly the center of gravity of world Christianity is shifting from Europe and the North to the peoples of the South—the poor of Latin America, Asia, and Africa, for whom God, as Gandhi used to say, must appear in the form of bread. If Christianity is to offer the bread of life, if it is to assume a global rather than merely imperial identity, it must attend carefully to the questions that Gandhi has posed. He reminds us of the Christ of the Untouchables, stripped to a loincloth, as he washed the feet of his disciples. If the memory leaves us feeling overdressed, so much the better.

Glossary

Ahimsa — nonviolence; love

Ashram — a spiritual community; one of Gandhi's colonies

Bhagavad Gita — a Hindu scripture, beloved of Gandhi; poetic discourses of Lord Krishna

Bramacharya — chastity, continence

Brahmin — the highest Hindu caste

Gita — see *Bhagavad Gita*

Harijans — lit. children of God, Gandhi's name for untouchables

Khadi — home-spun cloth, symbol of Gandhian movement

Mahatma — Great Soul, popular honorific title for Gandhi

Pariah — untouchable, Hindu outcaste

Satyagraha — lit. clinging to Truth; nonviolent resistance

Satyagrahi — a practitioner of *Satyagraha*

Swadeshi — self-reliance, the duty to serve one's neighbors by using local products

Swaraj — self-rule, Independence

PART ONE

GANDHI ON CHRISTIANITY

—— Chapter One ——

Encounters with Christianity

GLIMPSES OF RELIGION

Mohandas Karamchand Gandhi was born in 1869 in Porbandar, a port town in Gujarat in the western part of India. His family belonged to the Vaisya, or merchant, caste. His grandfather served as prime minister in the small principality of Rajkot, an office that fell in turn to his father when Gandhi was seven. The family religion was Vaishnava Hinduism, which centers on the god Vishnu. In his youth, however, Gandhi had little direct exposure to doctrine or scripture. The piety of his mother was the strongest religious influence of his childhood, along with a nurse, Rambha, who taught him to banish fears by repeating *Ramanama*, the name of God. In the following selections from his autobiography, *The Story of My Experiments with Truth*, Gandhi describes the religious atmosphere of his childhood and his early impressions of Christianity.

In Rajkot I got an early grounding in toleration for all branches of Hinduism and sister religions. For my father and mother would visit the *Haveli** and also Shiva's and Rama's temples, and would take or send us youngsters there. Jain monks also would pay frequent visits to my father, and would even go out of their way to accept food from us non-Jains. They would have talks with my father on subjects religious and mundane.

He had besides Mussalman** and Parsi friends, who would talk to him about their own faiths, and he would listen to them always with respect, and often with interest. Being his nurse, I often had a chance to be present at these talks. These many things combined to inculcate in me a toleration for all faiths.

Only Christianity was at the time an exception. I developed a sort of dislike for it. And for a reason. In those days Christian missionaries used

* *Haveli* refers to Vaishnava temple worship.
** That is, Muslim.

3

to stand in a corner near the high school and hold forth, pouring abuse on Hindus and their gods. I could not endure this. I must have stood there to hear them once only, but that was enough to dissuade me from repeating the experiment. About the same time, I heard of a well-known Hindu having been converted to Christianity. It was the talk of the town that, when he was baptized, he had to eat beef and drink liquor, that he also had to change his clothes, and that thenceforth he began to go about in European costume including a hat. These things got on my nerves. Surely, thought I, a religion that compelled one to eat beef, drink liquor, and change one's own clothes did not deserve the name. I also heard that the new convert had already begun abusing the religion of his ancestors, their customs, and their country. All these things created in me a dislike for Christianity. . . .

But one thing took deep root in me—the conviction that morality is the basis of things, and that truth is the substance of all morality. Truth became my sole objective. It began to grow in magnitude every day, and my definition of it also has been ever widening.

A Gujarati didactic stanza likewise gripped my mind and heart. Its precept—return good for evil—became my guiding principle. It became such a passion with me that I began numerous experiments in it. Here are those (for me) wonderful lines:

> For a bowl of water give a goodly meal;
> For a kindly greeting bow thou down with zeal;
> For a simple penny pay thou back with gold;
> If thy life be rescued, life do not withhold.
> Thus the words and actions of the wise regard;
> But the truly noble know all men as one,
> And return with gladness good for evil done.

The Story of My Experiments with Truth, Part I, Chap. X.

ACQUAINTANCE WITH RELIGIONS

In 1887 Gandhi traveled to London to study law. After a mediocre performance in school, it was felt by Gandhi's family that only a proper English education could secure the youth's fortune. Through his early contacts in the world of English vegetarianism, Gandhi encountered diverse religious movements, including Theosophy and other non-comformist philosophies, many of them influenced by the East. It was from these contacts that he was first introduced, in English translation, to such Hindu texts as the *Bhagavadgita.* It was also during this period that he made his first acquaintance with practicing Christians.

Towards the end of my second year in England I met a good Christian from Manchester in a vegetarian boarding house. He talked to me about

Christianity. I narrated to him my Rajkot recollections. He was pained to hear them. He said, "I am a vegetarian, I do not drink. Many Christians are meat-eaters and drink, no doubt; but neither meat-eating nor drinking is enjoined by Scripture. Do please read the Bible." I accepted his advice and he got me a copy. I have a faint recollection that he himself used to sell copies of the Bible, and I purchased from him an edition containing maps, concordance, and other aids. I began reading it, but I could not possibly read through the Old Testament. I read the book of Genesis, and the chapters that followed invariably sent me to sleep. But just for the sake of being able to say that I had read it, I plodded through the other books with much difficulty and without the least interest or understanding. I disliked reading the book of Numbers.

But the New Testament produced a different impression, especially the Sermon on the Mount which went straight to my heart. I compared it with the *Gita*. The verses, "But I say unto you, that ye resist not evil: but whosoever shall smite thee on thy right cheek, turn to him the other side also. And if any man take away thy coat let him have thy cloak too,"* delighted me beyond measure and put me in mind of Shamal Bhatt's "For a bowl of water, give a goodly meal," etc.

The Story of My Experiments with Truth, Part I, Chap. XX.

CHRISTIAN CONTACTS

In 1893 Gandhi arrived in South Africa to begin his career as a lawyer serving the Indian community. It was there that his experience of racial prejudice propelled him toward his first experiments in nonviolent struggle. At this point, Gandhi's knowledge of the world religions, including the Hinduism of his birth, was fairly superficial, and he was hospitable to the efforts of his Christian acquaintances to interest him in Christianity. A lawyer, Mr. A. W. Baker, who was also an evangelical lay preacher, invited him to participate in a prayer meeting.

The next day at one o'clock I went to Mr. Baker's prayer-meeting. There I was introduced to Miss Harris, Miss Gabb, Mr. Coates and others. Everyone kneeled down to pray and I followed suit. The prayers were supplications of God for various things, according to each person's desire. Thus the usual forms were for the day to be passed peacefully, or for God to open the doors of the heart.

A prayer was now added for my welfare: "Lord, show the path to the new brother, who has come amongst us. Give him, Lord, the peace that Thou hast given us. May the Lord Jesus who has saved us save him too. We ask all this in the name of Jesus." There was no singing of hymns or other music at these meetings. After the supplication for something special

* Matthew 5:39-40.

every day, we dispersed, each going to his lunch, that being the hour for it. The prayer did not take more than five minutes.

The Misses Harris and Gabb were both elderly maiden ladies. Mr. Coates was a Quaker. The two ladies lived together, and they gave me a standing invitation to four o'clock tea, at their house, every Sunday.

When we met on Sundays, I used to give Mr. Coates my religious diary for the week, and discuss with him the books I had read and the impression they had left on me. The ladies used to narrate their sweet experiences, and talk about the peace they had found.

Mr. Coates was a frank-hearted staunch young man. We went out for walks together, and he also took me to other Christian friends.

As we came closer to each other, he began to give me books of his own choice, until my shelf was filled with them. He loaded me with books, as it were. In pure faith I consented to read all those books, and as I went on reading them, we discussed them.

I read a number of such books in 1893. I do not remember the names of them all, but they included the *Commentary* of Dr. Parker of the City Temple, Pearson's *Many Infallible Proofs* and Butler's *Analogy*. Parts of these were unintelligible to me. I liked some things in them, while I did not like others. *Many Infallible Proofs* were proofs in support of the religion of the Bible as the author understood it. The book had no effect on me. Parker's *Commentary* was morally stimulating, but it could not be of any help to one who had no faith in the prevalent Christian beliefs. Butler's *Analogy* struck me to be a very profound and difficult book, which should be read four or five times to be understood properly. It seemed to me to be written with a view to converting atheists to theism. The arguments advanced in it regarding the existence of God were unnecessary for me, as I had then passed the stage of unbelief; but the arguments in proof of Jesus being the only incarnation of God and the Mediator between God and man left me unmoved.

But Mr. Coates was not the man easily to accept defeat. He had great affection for me. He saw, round my neck, the Vaishnava necklace of *Tulasi* beads. He thought it to be superstition, and was pained by it. "This super-stition does not become you. Come, let me break the necklace."

"No, you will not. It is a sacred gift from my mother." "But do you believe in it?" "I do not know its mysterious significance. I do not think I should come to harm if I did not wear it. But I cannot, without sufficient reason, give up a necklace that she put round my neck out of love and in the conviction that it would be conducive to my welfare. When, with the passage of time, it wears away and breaks of its own accord, I shall have no desire to get a new one. But this necklace cannot be broken."

Mr. Coates could not appreciate my argument, as he had no regard for my religion. He was looking forward to delivering me from the abyss of ignorance. He wanted to convince me that, no matter whether there was some truth in other religions, salvation was impossible for me unless I accepted Christianity which represented the truth, and that my sins would not be washed away except by the intercession of Jesus, and that all good works were useless.

Just as he introduced me to several books, he introduced me to several friends whom he regarded as staunch Christians. One of these introductions was to a family which belonged to the Plymouth Brethren, a Christian sect.*

Many of the contacts for which Mr. Coates was responsible were good. Most struck me as being God-fearing. But during my contact with this family, one of the Plymouth Brethren confronted me with an argument for which I was not prepared.

"You cannot understand the beauty of our religion. From what you say it appears that you must be brooding over your transgressions every moment of your life, always mending them and atoning for them. How can this ceaseless cycle of action bring you redemption? You can never have peace. You admit that we are all sinners. Now look at the perfection of our belief. Our attempts at improvement and atonement are futile. And yet redemption we must have. How can we bear the burden of sin? We can but throw it on Jesus. He is the only sinless Son of God. It is His word that those who believe in Him shall have everlasting life. Therein lies God's infinite mercy. And as we believe in the atonement of Jesus, our own sins do not bind us. Sin we must. It is impossible to live in this world sinless. And therefore Jesus suffered and atoned for all the sins of mankind. Only he who accepts His great redemption can have eternal peace. Think what a life of restlessness is yours, and what a promise of peace we have."

The argument utterly failed to convince me. I humbly replied:

"If this be the Christianity acknowledged by all Christians, I cannot accept it. I do not seek redemption from the consequences of my sin. I seek to be redeemed from sin itself, or rather from the very thought of sin. Until I have attained that end, I shall be content to be restless."

To which the Plymouth Brother rejoined: "I assure you your attempt is fruitless. Think again over what I have said."

And the Brother proved as good as his word. He knowingly committed transgressions and showed me that he was undisturbed by the thought of them.

But I already knew before meeting with these friends that all Christians did not believe in such a theory of atonement. Mr. Coates himself walked in the fear of God. His heart was pure, and he believed in the possibility of self-purification. The two ladies also shared this belief. Some of the books that came into my hands were full of devotion. So although Mr. Coates was very much disturbed by this latest experience of mine, I was able to reassure him and tell him that the distorted belief of a Plymouth Brother could not prejudice me against Christianity.

---

* The Plymouth Brethren are a conservative Protestant evangelical sect which began in the 1820s in England.

My difficulties lay elsewhere. They were with regard to the Bible and its accepted interpretation.

The Story of My Experiments with Truth, Part II, Chap. XI.

RELIGIOUS FERMENT

Mr. Baker was getting anxious about my future. He took me to the Wellington Convention. The Protestant Christians organize such gatherings every few years for religious enlightenment or, in other words, self-purification. One may call this religious restoration or revival. The Wellington Convention was of this type. The chairman was the famous divine of the place, the Rev. Andrew Murray. Mr. Baker had hoped that the atmosphere of religious exaltation at the Convention, and the enthusiasm and earnestness of the people attending it would inevitably lead me to embrace Christianity.

But his final hope was the efficacy of prayer. He had an abiding faith in prayer. It was his firm conviction that God could not but listen to prayer fervently offered. He would cite the instances of men like George Muller of Bristol, who depended entirely on prayer even for his temporal needs. I listened to his discourse on the efficacy of prayer with unbiased attention, and assured him that nothing could prevent me from embracing Christianity, should I feel the call. I had no hesitation in giving him this assurance, as I had long since taught myself to follow the inner voice. I delighted in submitting to it. To act against it would be difficult and painful to me.

So we went to Wellington.

This Convention was an assemblage of devout Christians. I was delighted at their faith. I met the Rev. Murray. I saw that many were praying for me. I liked some of their hymns, they were very sweet.

The Convention lasted for three days. I could understand and appreciate the devoutness of those who attended it. But I saw no reason for changing my belief — my religion. It was impossible for me to believe that I could go to heaven or attain salvation only by becoming a Christian. When I frankly said so to some of the good Christian friends, they were shocked. But there was no help for it.

My difficulties lay deeper. It was more than I could believe that Jesus was the only incarnate son of God, and that only he who believed in Him would have everlasting life. If God could have sons, all of us were his sons. If Jesus was like God, or God Himself, then all men were like God and could be God Himself. My reason was not ready to believe literally that Jesus by his death and by his blood redeemed the sins of the world. Metaphorically there might be some truth in it. Again, according to Christianity only human beings had souls, and not other living beings, for whom death meant complete extinction; while I held a contrary belief. I could accept Jesus as a martyr, an embodiment of sacrifice, and a divine teacher, but not as the most perfect man ever born. His death on the Cross was a great example to the world, but that there was anything like a mysterious or miraculous virtue in it, my heart could not accept. The pious lives of Christians did not give me anything that the lives of men of other faiths had failed to give. I had seen in other lives just the same reformation that I had heard of among Christians. Philosophically there was nothing extraordinary in Christian principles. From the point of view of sacrifice, it seemed to me that the Hindus greatly surpassed the Christians. It was impossible for me to regard Christianity as a perfect religion or the greatest of all religions.

I shared this mental churning with my Christian friends whenever there was an opportunity, but their answers could not satisfy me.

Thus if I could not accept Christianity either as a perfect, or the greatest, religion, neither was I then convinced of Hinduism being such. Hindu defects were pressingly visible to me. If untouchability could be a part of Hinduism, it could but be a rotten part or an excrescence. I could not understand the raison d'être of a multitude of sects and castes. What was the meaning of saying that the Vedas were the inspired Word of God? If they were inspired, why not also the Bible and the Koran?

As Christian friends were endeavouring to convert me, even so were Mussalman friends. Abdulla Sheth* had kept on inducing me to study Islam, and of course he had always something to say regarding its beauty.

I expressed my difficulties in a letter to Raychandbhai.** I also corresponded with other religious authorities in India and received answers from them. Raychandbhai's letter somewhat pacified me. He asked me to be patient and to study Hinduism more deeply. One of his sentences was to this effect: "On a dispassionate view of the question, I am convinced that no other religion has the subtle and profound thought of Hinduism, its vision of the soul, or its charity."

I purchased Sale's translation of the Koran and began reading it. I also obtained other books on Islam. I communicated with Christian friends in England. One of them introduced me to Edward Maitland,† with whom I opened correspondence. He sent me *The Perfect Way,* a book he had written in collaboration with Anna Kingsford. The book was a repudiation of the current Christian belief. He also sent me another book, *The New Interpretation of the Bible.* I liked both. They seemed to support Hinduism. Tolstoy's *The Kingdom of God is Within You*†† overwhelmed me. It left an abiding

---

* Abdulla Sheth, a Muslim businessman, was Gandhi's employer in South Africa.
** Raychandbhai was a Jaina intellectual in Bombay whom Gandhi frequently consulted on religious matters. In his autobiography he writes, "Three moderns have left a deep impress on my life, and captivated me: Raychandbhai by his living contact; Tolstoy by his book, *The Kingdom of God is Within You*; and Ruskin by his *Unto this Last.*"
† Maitland was the founder of the Esoteric Christian Union.
†† Leo Tolstoy's book was published in English in 1894. It contains Tolstoy's pacifist interpretation of the Sermon on the Mount, which left a deep influence on Gandhi's philosophy of nonviolence. Gandhi subsequently initiated a correspondence with Tolstoy that lasted until the latter's death in 1910.

impression on me. Before the independent thinking, profound morality, and the truthfulness of this book, all the books given me by Mr. Coates seemed to pale into insignificance.

My studies thus carried me in a direction unthought of by my Christian friends. My correspondence with Edward Maitland was fairly prolonged, and that with Raychandbhai continued until his death. . . .

Though I took a path my Christian friends had not intended for me, I have remained forever indebted to them for the religious quest that they awakened in me. I shall always cherish the memory of their contact. The years that followed had more, not less, of such sweet and sacred contacts in store for me.

The Story of My Experiments with Truth, Part II, Chap. XV.

COMPARATIVE STUDY OF RELIGIONS

Gandhi had arrived in South Africa with the intention of gaining experience as a lawyer before returning to India. Drawn into the struggle for Indian civil rights, he ended up remaining in South Africa for twenty years. It was in South Africa that he committed himself to the pursuit of consistent nonviolence as a way of life. At the same time, his encounters with Christians and his earnest efforts to appreciate their religion left him confirmed in his Hindu faith. Henceforward the struggle for justice was inseparable for Gandhi from the search for God.

Christian friends had whetted my appetite for knowledge which had become almost insatiable, and they would not leave me in peace, even if I desired to be indifferent. In Durban Mr. Spencer Walton, the head of the South Africa General Mission, found me out. I became almost a member of his family. At the back of this acquaintance was of course my contact with Christians in Pretoria. Mr. Walton had a manner all his own. I do not recollect his ever having invited me to embrace Christianity. But he placed his life as an open book before me, and let me watch all his movements. Mrs. Walton was a very gentle and talented woman. I liked the attitude of this couple. We knew the fundamental differences between us. Any amount of discussion could not efface them. Yet even differences prove helpful, where there are tolerance, charity, and truth. I liked Mr. and Mrs. Walton's humility, perseverance, and devotion to work, and we met very frequently.

This friendship kept alive my interest in religion. It was impossible now to get the leisure that I used to have in Pretoria for my religious studies. But what little time I could spare I turned to good account. My religious correspondence continued. Raychandbhai was guiding me. . . .

Thus I gained more knowledge of the different religions. The study stimulated my self-introspection, and fostered in me the habit of putting into practice whatever appealed to me in my studies. Thus I began some of the Yogic practices, as well as I could understand them from a reading of Hindu books. But I could not get on very far, and decided to follow them with the help of some expert when I returned to India. The desire has never been fulfilled.

I made too an intensive study of Tolstoy's books. *The Gospels in Brief, What to Do?*, and other books made a deep impression on me. I began to realize more and more the infinite possibilities of universal love.

About the same time I came in contact with another Christian family. At their suggestion, I attended the Wesleyan Church every Sunday. For these days I also had their standing invitation to dinner. The church did not make a favorable impression on me. The sermons seemed to be uninspiring. The congregation did not strike me as being particularly religious. They were not an assembly of devout souls; they appeared rather to be worldly-minded people going to church for recreation and in conformity to custom. Here, at times, I would involuntarily doze. I was ashamed, but some of my neighbors, who were in no better case, lightened the shame. I could not go on long like this, and soon gave up attending the service.

My connection with the family I used to visit every Sunday was abruptly broken. In fact it may be said that I was warned to visit it no more. It happened thus. My hostess was a good and simple woman, but somewhat narrow-minded. We always discussed religious subjects. I was then rereading Arnold's *Light of Asia.** Once we began to compare the life of Jesus with that of Buddha. "Look at Gautama's compassion!" said I. "It was not confined to mankind, it was extended to all living beings. Does not one's heart overflow with love to think of the lamb joyously perched on his shoulders? One fails to notice this love for all living beings in the life of Jesus." The comparison pained the good lady. I could understand her feelings. I cut the matter short, and we went to the dining room. Her son, a cherub aged scarcely five, was also with us. I am happiest when in the midst of children, and this youngster and I had long been friends. I spoke derisively of the piece of meat on his plate and in high praise of the apple on mine. The innocent boy was carried away and joined in my praise of the fruit.

But the mother? She was dismayed.

I was warned. I checked myself and changed the subject. The following week I visited the family as usual, but not without trepidation. I did not see that I should stop going there. I did not think it proper either. But the good lady made my way easy.

"Mr. Gandhi," she said, "please don't take it ill if I feel obliged to tell you that my boy is none the better for your company. Every day he hesitates to eat meat and asks for fruit, reminding me of your argument. This is too much. If he gives up meat, he is bound to get weak, if not ill. How could I bear it? Your discussions should henceforth be only with us elders. They are sure to react badly on children."

"Mrs. —," I replied, "I am sorry. I can understand your feelings as a parent, for I too have children. We can very easily end this unpleasant state

* *The Light of Asia* by Sir Edwin Arnold is a poetic re-telling of the life of (Gautama) Buddha.

of things. What I eat and omit to eat is bound to have a greater effect on the child than what I say. The best way, therefore, is for me to stop these visits. That certainly need not affect our friendship."

"I thank you," she said with evident relief.

The Story of My Experiments with Truth, Part II, Chap. XXII.

WHY I DID NOT BECOME A CHRISTIAN

Gandhi's interlocutor here, Millie Polak, was the wife of Henry Polak, a Jewish vegetarian from England who became one of Gandhi's earliest disciples in South Africa. Mrs. Polak, who was a Christian, lived with her husband, the Gandhis, and several other familiies at Phoenix Farm, an experimental Tolstoyan community in Johannesburg.

Gandhi: I did once seriously think of embracing the Christian faith. The gentle figure of Christ, so patient, so kind, so loving, so full of forgiveness that he taught his followers not to retaliate when abused or struck, but to turn the other cheek. I thought it was a beautiful example of the perfect man.

Mrs. Polak: But you did not embrace Christianity, did you?

Gandhi: No. I studied your Scriptures for some time and thought earnestly about them. I was tremendously attracted to Christianity, but, eventually, I came to the conclusion that there was nothing really in your Scriptures that we had not got in ours, and that to be a good Hindu also meant that I would be a good Christian. There was no need for me to join your creed to be a believer in the beauty of the teachings of Jesus or to try to follow his example.

Mrs. Polak: Of course, it is what a man is that counts, not what he calls himself. But, tell me, do you believe in conversion, in changing from one form of faith to another?

Gandhi: What do you feel yourself?

Mrs. Polak: It does not please me, somehow. I could not do it.

Gandhi: I think that is right. If a man reaches the heart of his own religion, he has reached the heart of the others, too. There is only one God, but there are many paths to Him.

Mrs. Polak: If Karma and reincarnation be true, we are born into the faith to which we belong, and the one most suitable at the moment for our development. So, we should not change.

Gandhi: What do you think is the essential lesson for man in the teaching of Christianity?

Mrs. Polak: I could think of two or three. But the one that stands out strongest in my mind at the moment is *Love*, which is expressed in the words: "One is your Master, Christ, and all ye are brethren."

Gandhi: Yes, and Hinduism teaches the same great truth, and Mohammedanism and Zoroastrianism, too.

Mrs. Polak: Do you think Hinduism does teach "all men are brothers" as Christianity does?

Gandhi: Do not take men's imperfect interpretation, as you see it, for the real teaching of any great faith. You would not suggest to me that the Christian world lives as brothers, would you? Think of its wars, its hatred, its poverty and its crime.

Mrs. Polak: That is true. I suppose the ideals of mankind are always far ahead of them, and men and women are very much the same in whatever part of the world you find them.

Gandhi: If we realized our ideals, they would cease to be ideals. We should have nothing to strive for.

Mr. Gandhi: The Man, p. 40.

PROSELYTIZATION

Charles Freer Andrews, "Charlie," as Gandhi called him, was a Christian missionary and pacifist who first met Gandhi in South Africa and became a lifelong friend. He wrote one of the earliest biographies of Gandhi who, in turn, often commended Andrews as a model for other Christians.

C. F. Andrews: What would you say to a man who, after considerable thought and prayer, said that he could not have his peace and salvation except by becoming a Christian?

Gandhi: I would say that, if a non-Christian (say a Hindu) came to a Christian and made that statement, he should ask him to become a good Hindu rather than find goodness in change of faith.

Andrews: I cannot in this go the whole length with you, though you know my own position. I discarded the position that there is no salvation except through Christ long ago. But supposing the Oxford Group Movement* people changed the life of your son, and he felt like being converted, what would you say?

Gandhi: I would say that the Oxford Group may change the lives of as many as they like, but not their religion. They can draw their attention to the best in their respective religions, and change their lives by asking them to live according to them. There came to me a man, the son of Brahmin parents, who said his reading of your book had led him to embrace Christianity. I asked him if he thought that the religion of his forefathers was wrong. He said: "No." Then, I said: "Is there any difficulty about your accepting the Bible as one of the great religious books of the world and Christ as one of the great teachers?" I said to him that you had never through your books asked Indians to take up the Bible and embrace Christianity, and that he had misread your book—unless, of course, your position

* A Christian missionary society based in England.

is like that of the late Maulana Mohammed Ali's*, viz., that a believing Mussalman, however bad his life, is better than a good Hindu.

Andrews: I do not accept M. Mohammed Ali's position at all. But I do say that if a person really needs a chance of faith, I should not stand in his way.

Gandhi: But don't you see that you do not even give him a chance? You do not even cross-examine him. Supposing a Christian came to me and said he was captivated by reading of the *Bhagavat* and so wanted to declare himself a Hindu, I should say to him: "No. What the *Bhagavat* offers, the Bible also offers. You have not yet made the attempt to find out. Make the attempt and be a good Christian."

Andrews: I don't know. If someone earnestly says that he will become a good Christian, I should say: "You may become one," though you know that I have in my own life strongly dissuaded ardent enthusiasts who came to me. I said to them: "Certainly, not on my account will you do anything of the kind. But human nature does require a concrete faith.

Gandhi: If a person wants to believe in the Bible, let him say so, but why should he disregard his own religion? This proselytization will mean no peace in the world. Religion is a very personal matter. We should, by living the life according to our lights, share the best with one another, thus adding to the sum total of human effort to reach God.

Consider whether you are going to accept the position of mutual toleration or of equality of all religions. My position is that all the great religions are fundamentally equal. We must have the innate respect for other religions as we have for our own. Mind you, not mutual toleration, but equal respect.

Harijan, November 28, 1936

A HOT GOSPELLER

Lady Emily Kinnaird, an English woman devoted equally to the Y.M.C.A. and India, was eighty-six at the time of this interview with Gandhi. Their conversation began with a discussion of Denmark's passive resistance to Hitler's invasion.

Lady Emily: Don't you think Denmark has carried out your idea of nonviolence?

Gandhi: Not a bit. It was a surrender, and what I have asked for is not surrender, but nonviolent resistance.

Lady Emily: But Denmark did not resist and did exactly as you have advised Britons today!

Gandhi: But I have not asked for unresisting surrender or capitulation. I have appealed to Britons and everyone in their plight to display the

* Mohammed Ali and his brother Shaukat were early Muslim collaborators with Gandhi in the Indian independence movement. Ultimately, their loyalties shifted toward the Muslim nationalist cause.

highest courage that man is capable of, viz., to refuse to use arms and to defy the enemy to walk over their dead bodies. Denmark did nothing of the kind.

Lady Emily: But Denmark had no time. It was all so sudden and there was nothing for it but for her to offer no resistance.

Gandhi: I know. I know. But it is such suddenness that puts nonviolence to the test. It was no doubt prudent on her part to offer no resistance. But prudence is not the same thing as nonviolence. Nonviolent resistance is far more effective than violent resistance, and that is what I have asked for from these nations which are so accustomed to violent resistance.

Lady Emily: Well, well, what's the good of it?

Gandhi: What was the good of Jesus Christ laying down His life?

Lady Emily: Oh, that was a different matter. He was the son of God.

Gandhi: And so are we!

Lady Emily: No. He was the *only* son of God.

Gandhi: It is there that the mother and son must differ. With you, Jesus was the only begotten son of God. With me, He was a son of God, no matter how much purer than us all, but every one of us is a son of God and capable of doing what Jesus did, if we but endeavor to express the Divine in us.

Lady Emily: Yes, that is where I think you are wrong. If you accepted Christ in your heart and appealed to your people to do likewise, you could deliver your message with greater ease and far better effect. He is our salvation, and without receiving Him in our hearts we cannot be saved.

Gandhi: So those who accept the Christ are all saved. They need do nothing more?

Lady Emily: We are sinners all, and we have but to accept Him to be saved.

Gandhi: And, then, we may continue to be sinners? Is that what you mean? You do not happen to belong to the Plymouth Brothers, do you?

Lady Emily: No, I am a Presbyterian.

Gandhi: But you talk like some of the Plymouth Brothers I met long ago in South Africa.

Lady Emily: Yes, I am afraid you were so unfortunate in the Christian contacts you formed in South Africa. You did not meet the right kind of people.

Gandhi: Surely, you will not say that. I met a number of estimable people. They were all honest and sincere.

Lady Emily: But they were not *true* Christians.

Gandhi: Do you know F. W. Meyer?

Lady Emily: Oh yes.

Gandhi: Well, then, let me tell you that it was F. W. Meyer who, after a long talk with me, asked the other Christian friends to let me alone. He said to them that I was as good as converted, and that I did not need any formal process of conversion. But, of course, that did not satisfy them. And old A. W. Baker, who must be much over eighty now, is still at me. He writes to remind me time and again that, unless I accept Christ in his way, I cannot be saved.

But why all this quarrel about labels? Cannot a few hundred thousand Indians or Africans live the message of Christ without being called Christians?

Lady Emily: No, for without the grace of Jesus one cannot be saved. One has to accept Christ in one's heart. That is the definition of a true Christian, and I admit there are few Christians today.

Harijan, August 4, 1940

—— Chapter Two ——

The Message of Jesus

THE GREATEST ECONOMIST OF HIS TIME

Gandhi returned to India in 1915 and soon thereafter plunged into action on behalf of the Indian National Congress and the struggle for independence. Critical of the elitism of many Congress leaders, he was determined, from the beginning, to link independence with the cause of the poor. The following remarks are taken from a lecture delivered by Gandhi at a meeting of the Muir Central College Economic Society in Allahabad on December 22, 1916.

"Take no thought for the morrow" is an injunction which finds an echo in almost all the religious scriptures of the world. In a well-ordered society the securing of one's livelihood should be and is found to be the easiest thing in the world. *Indeed, the test of orderliness in a country is not the number of millionaires it owns, but the absence of starvation among its masses.* The only statement that has to be examined is, whether it can be laid down as a law of universal application that *material advancement means moral progress.*

Now let us take a few illustrations. Rome suffered a moral fall when it attained high material affluence. So did Egypt and perhaps most countries of which we have any historical record. The descendants and kinsmen of the royal and divine Krishna too fell when they were rolling in riches. We do not deny to the Rockefellers and Carnegies possession of an ordinary measure of morality but we gladly judge them indulgently. I mean that we do not even expect them to satisfy the highest standard of morality. With them material gain has not necessarily meant moral gain. In South Africa, where I had the privilege of associating with thousands of our countrymen on most intimate terms, I observed almost invariably that the greater the possession of riches, the greater was their moral turpitude. Our rich men, to say the least, did not advance the moral struggle of passive resistance as did the poor. The rich men's sense of self-respect was not so much injured as that of the poorest. If I were not afraid of treading on dangerous ground,

17

I would even come nearer home and show how that possession of riches has been a hindrance to real growth. I venture to think that the scriptures of the world are far safer and sounder treatises on the laws of economics than many of the modern textbooks. The question we are asking ourselves ... is not a new one. It was addressed by Jesus two thousand years ago.

St. Mark has vividly described the scene. Jesus is in his solemn mood. He is earnest. He talks of eternity. He knows the world about him. He is himself the greatest economist of his time. He succeeded in economizing time and space — he transcends them. It is to him at his best that one comes running, kneels down, and asks: "Good Master, what shall I do that I may inherit eternal life?" And Jesus said unto him: "Why callest thou me good? There is none good but one, that is God. Thou knowest the commandments. Do not commit adultery. Do not kill, do not steal, do not bear false witness. Defraud not, honor thy Father and Mother." And he answered and said unto him: "Master, all these have I observed from my youth." Then Jesus beholding him loved him and said unto him: "One thing thou lackest. Go thy way, sell whatever thou hast and give to the poor, and thou shalt have treasure in heaven — *come*, take up the cross *and follow me.*" And he was sad at that saying and went away grieved — for he had great possession. And Jesus looked round about and said unto the disciples: "How hardly shall they that have riches enter into the kingdom of God." And the disciples were astonished at his words. But Jesus answereth again and said unto them: "Children, how hard is it for them that trust in riches to enter into the kingdom of God. It is easier for a camel to go through the eye of a needle than for a rich man to enter into the kingdom of God!"

Here you have an eternal rule of life stated in the noblest words the English language is capable of producing. But the disciples nodded unbelief as we do to this day. To him they said as we say today: "But look how the law fails in practice. If we sell and have nothing, we shall have nothing to eat. We must have money or we cannot even be reasonably moral." So they state their case thus. And they were astonished out of measure, saying among themselves: "Who then can be saved?" And Jesus looking upon them said: "With men it is impossible, but not with God, for with God, all things are possible." Then Peter began to say unto him: "Lo, we have left all, and have followed thee." And Jesus answered and said: "Verily I say unto you, there is no man that has left house or brethren or sisters, or father or mother, or wife or children or lands for my sake but he shall receive one hundredfold, now in this time houses and brethren and sisters and mothers and children and land, and in the world to come, eternal life. But many that are first shall be last and the last, first."

You have here the result or reward, if you prefer the term, of following the law. I have not taken the trouble of copying similar passages from the other non-Hindu scriptures and I will not insult you by quoting, in support of the law stated by Jesus, passages from the writings and sayings of our own sages, passages even stronger, if possible, than the biblical extracts I have drawn to your attention. Perhaps the strongest of all the testimonies in favor of the affirmative answer to the question before us are the lives of the greatest teachers of the world; Jesus, Mahomed, Buddha, Nank, Kabir, Chaitanya, Shankara, Dayanand, Ramakrishna were men who exercised an immense influence over, and moulded the character of thousands of men. The world is the richer for their having lived in it. And they were all men who deliberately embraced poverty as their lot. . . .

We need not be afraid of ideals or of reducing them to practice even to the uttermost. Ours will only then be a truly spiritual nation when we shall show more truth than gold, greater fearlessness than pomp of power and wealth, greater charity than love of self. If we will but clean our houses, our palaces, and temples of the attributes of wealth and show in them the attributes of morality, we can offer battle to any combinations of hostile forces without having to carry the burden of a heavy militia. Let us seek first the Kingdom of God and His righteousness, and the irrevocable promise is that everything will be added upon us. These are real economics. May you and I treasure them and enforce them in our daily life.

Speeches and Writings of Mahatma Gandhi
(Madras: Natesan & Co., 1933), pp. 255-61

MY OPINION ON CHRISTIANITY

The following address was delivered at the Young Men's Christian Association (YMCA) in Colombo, Ceylon, in 1927.

The message of Jesus, as I understand it, is contained in His Sermon on the Mount unadulterated and taken as a whole, and even in connection with the Sermon on the Mount, my own humble interpretation of the message is in many respects different from the orthodox. The message, to my mind, has suffered distortion in the West. It may be presumptuous for me to say so, but as a devotee of truth, I should not hesitate to say what I feel. I know that the world is not waiting to know my opinion on Christianity.

One's own religion is after all a matter between oneself and one's Maker and no one else's, but if I feel impelled to share my thoughts with you this evening, it is because I want to enlist your sympathy in my search for truth and because so many Christian friends are interested in my thoughts on the teachings of Jesus. If then I had to face only the Sermon on the Mount and my own interpretation of it, I should not hesitate to say, "Oh yes, I am a Christian." But I know that at the present moment if I said any such thing I would lay myself open to the gravest misinterpretation. I should lay myself open to fraudulent claims because I would have then to tell you what my own meaning of Christianity is, and I have no desire myself to give you my own view of Christianity. But negatively I can tell you that, in my humble opinion, much of what passes as Christianity is a negation of the Sermon on the Mount. And please mark my words. I am not at the present moment speaking of the Christian conduct. I am speaking of the Christian belief, of Christianity as it is understood in the West. I am painfully aware of the fact that conduct everywhere falls short of belief. But I don't say this by way of criticism. I know from the treasures of my own experience that, although I am every moment of my life trying to live up to my professions, my conduct falls short of these professions. Far, therefore, be it from me to say this in a spirit of criticism. But I am placing before you my fundamental difficulties.

When I began as a prayerful student to study the Christian literature in South Africa in 1893, I asked myself "Is this Christianity?" and have always got the Vedic answer, "Neti, Neti" (not this, not this), and the deepest in me tells me that I am right.

I claim to be a man of faith and prayer, and even if I was cut to pieces, God would give me the strength not to deny Him and to assert that He is. The Muslim says: He is and there is no one else. The Christian says the same thing and so the Hindu, and, if I may say so, even the Buddhist says the same thing, if in different words. We may each of us be putting our own interpretation on the word God — God who embraces not only this tiny globe of ours, but millions and billions of such globes. How can we, little crawling creatures, so utterly helpless as He has made us, how could we possibly measure His greatness, His boundless love, His infinite compassion, such that He allows man insolently to deny Him, wrangle about Him, and cut the throat of his fellow-man? How can we measure the greatness of God who is so forgiving, so divine? Thus, though we may utter the same words they have not the same meaning for us all. And hence I say that we do not need to proselytize through our speech or writing. We can only do it really with our lives. Let them be open books for all to study. Would that I could persuade the missionary friends to take this view of their mission. Then there will be no distrust, no suspicion, no jealousy and no dissensions.

Young India, December 8, 1927

THINGS OF THE SPIRIT

One of the missionary friends wanted to know how the Gita and the New Testament compared as sources of comfort so far as Gandhiji was concerned, and instead of giving a bald answer that he derived all the comfort that he needed from the Bhagavadgita, he retold the story of the beginnings of his religious studies in England, with which the readers of the Autobiography are in the main familiar. All missionaries seem to forget that the men they approach with their gospel have their traditions and their own religion which sustain them from generation to generation. Gandhiji told these friends that when he read the Sermon on the Mount he read nothing new, but found in it, vividly told, what he had learnt in his childhood. "There is nothing much in giving a cup of water to one who gave you a cup of water, or saluting one who salutes you, but there is some virtue in doing a good turn to one who has done you a bad turn."

"I have not been able to see," he said, "any difference between the Sermon on the Mount and the Bhagavadgita. What the Sermon describes in a graphic manner, the Bhagavadgita reduces to a scientific formula. It may not be a scientific book in the accepted sense of the term, but it has argued out the law of love—the law of abandon as I would call it—in a scientific manner. The Sermon on the Mount gives the same law in wonderful language. The New Testament gave me comfort and boundless joy, as it came after the repulsion that parts of the Old had given me. Today supposing I was deprived of the Gita and forgot all its contents but had a copy of the Sermon, I should derive the same joy from it as I do from the Gita."

And as though summing up the argument with a great warning, he said, "You know there is one thing in me, and that is that I love to see the bright side of things and not the seamy side, and so I can derive comfort and inspiration from any great book of any great religion. I may not be able to reproduce a single verse from the Gita or the New Testament, a Hindu child or Christian child may be able to repeat the verses better, but those clever children cannot deprive me of the assimilation that is in me today of the spirit of the two books."

Mahadev Desai in, Young India, December 22, 1927

THE JESUS I LOVE

At the request of Christian fellow-passengers, Gandhi gave the following talk on Christmas Day, 1931, while sailing back to India after attending the Second Round Table Conference in London.

I shall tell you how, to an outsider like me, the story of Christ, as told in the New Testament, has struck. My acquaintance with the Bible began nearly forty-five years ago, and that was through the New Testament. I could not then take much interest in the Old Testament, which I had certainly read, if only to fulfill a promise I had made to a friend whom I happened to meet in a hotel. But when I came to the New Testament and the Sermon on the Mount, I began to understand the Christian teaching, and the teaching of the Sermon on the Mount echoed something I had learnt in childhood and something which seemed to be part of my being and which I felt was being acted up to in the daily life around me.

I say it seemed to be acted up to, meaning thereby that it was not necessary for my purpose that all were actually living the life. This teaching was nonretaliation, or nonresistance to evil. Of all the things I read, what remained with me for ever was that Jesus came almost to give a new law— though he of course had said he had not come to give a new law, but tack something on to the old Mosaic law. Well, he changed it so that it became a new law—not an eye for an eye, and a tooth for a tooth, but to be ready to receive two blows when only one was given, and to go two miles when they were asked to go one.

I said to myself, this is what one learns in one's childhood. Surely this is not Christianity. For all I had then been given to understand was that to be a Christian was to have a brandy bottle in one hand and beef in the other. The Sermon on the Mount, however, falsified the impression. As my contact with real Christians, i.e., men living in fear of God, increased, I saw that the Sermon on the Mount was the whole of Christianity for him who wanted to live a Christian life. It is that Sermon which has endeared Jesus to me.

I may say that I have never been interested in a historical Jesus. I should not care if it was proved by someone that the man called Jesus never lived, and that what was narrated in the Gospels was a figment of the writer's imagination. For the Sermon on the Mount would still be true for me.

Reading, therefore, the whole story in that light, it seems to me that Christianity has yet to be lived, unless one says that where there is boundless love and no idea of retaliation whatsoever, it is Christianity that lives. But then it surmounts all boundaries and book teaching. Then it is something indefinable, not capable of being preached to men, not capable of being transmitted from mouth to mouth, but from heart to heart. But Christianity is not commonly understood in that way.

Somehow, in God's providence, the Bible has been preserved from destruction by the Christians, so-called. The British and Foreign Bible Society has had it translated into many languages. All that may serve a real purpose in the time to come. Two thousand years in the life of a living faith may be nothing. For though we sang, "All glory to God on High and on the earth be peace," there seems to be today neither glory to God nor peace on earth.

As long as it remains a hunger still unsatisfied, as long as Christ is not yet born, we have to look forward to Him. When real peace is established, we will not need demonstrations, but it will be echoed in our life, not only in individual life, but in corporate life. Then we shall say Christ is born. That to me is the real meaning of the verse we have sung. Then we will not think of a particular day in the year as that of the birth of the Christ, but as an ever-recurring event which can be enacted in every life.

And the more I think of fundamental religion, and the more I think of miraculous conceptions of so many teachers who have come down from age to age and clime to clime, the more I see that there is behind them the eternal truth that I have narrated. That needs no label or declaration. It consists in the living of life, never ceasing, ever progressing towards peace.

When, therefore, one wishes "A Happy Christmas" without the meaning behind it, it becomes nothing more than an empty formula. And unless one wishes for peace for all life, one cannot wish for peace for oneself. It is a self-evident axiom, like the axioms of Euclid, that one cannot have peace unless there is in one an intense longing for peace all around. You may certainly experience peace in the midst of strife, but that happens only when to remove strife you destroy your whole life, you crucify yourself.

And so, as the miraculous birth is an eternal event, so is the Cross an eternal event in this stormy life. Therefore, we dare not think of birth without death on the cross. Living Christ means a living Cross, without it life is a living death.

[At the request of an American reporter, Gandhi added the following message of Christmas greetings].

I have never been able to reconcile myself to the gaieties of the Christmas season. They have appeared to me to be so inconsistent with the life and teaching of Jesus.

How I wish America could lead the way by devoting the season to a real moral stocktaking and emphasizing consecration to the service of mankind for which Jesus lived and died on the Cross.

Young India, December 31, 1931

THE PLACE OF JESUS

For many, many years I have regarded Jesus of Nazareth as one amongst the mighty teachers that the world has had, and I say this in all humility. I claim humility for this expression for the simple reason that this is exactly what I feel. Of course, Christians claim a higher place for Jesus of Nazareth than as a non-Christian and as a Hindu I have been able to feel. I purposely use the word "feel" instead of "give," because I consider that neither I, nor anybody else, can possibly arrogate to himself the claim of giving place to a great man.

The great teachers of mankind have had the places not given to them. But the place has belonged to them as a matter of right, as a matter of service that they have rendered; but it is given to the lowest and humblest amongst us to feel certain things about certain people. The relation between great teachers and ourselves is somewhat after the style of relation between a husband and wife. It would be a most terrible thing, a tragic thing, if I were to argue out intellectually for myself what place I was to give to my wife in my heart. It is not in my giving, but she takes the place that belongs to her as a matter of right in my heart. It is a matter purely for feeling.

Then, I can say that Jesus occupies in my heart the place of one of the great teachers who have made a considerable influence on my life. Leave the Christians alone for the present. I shall say to the Hindus that your lives will be incomplete unless you reverently study the teachings of Jesus. I have come to the conclusion, in my own experience, that those who, no matter to what faith they belong, reverently study the teaching of other faiths, broaden their own instead of narrowing their hearts. Personally, I do not regard any of the great religions of the world as false. All have served in enriching mankind and are now even serving their purpose.

There is one thing which occurs to me, which came to me in my early studies of the Bible. It seized me immediately I read the passage: "Make this world the Kingdom of God and His righteousness and everything will be added unto you." I tell you that if you will understand, appreciate, and act up to the spirit of this passage, you won't even need to know what place Jesus or any other teacher occupies in your heart. If you will do the proper scavenger's work, clean and purify your hearts and get them ready, you will find that all these mighty teachers take their places with our invitation from us.

Gandhi in Ceylon, p. 143

"THE LETTER KILLETH"

"The letter killeth, the spirit giveth life." My very first reading of the Bible showed me that I would be repelled by many things in it, if I gave their literal meaning to many texts or even took every passage in it as the word of God. I found, as I proceeded with my study of the scriptures of the various religions, that every scripture had to be treated likewise, not excepting the Vedas or the Upanishads. Therefore, the story of the Immaculate Conception, when I interpret it mystically, does not repel me. I should find it hard to believe in the literal meaning of the verses relating to the Immaculate Conception of Jesus. Nor would it deepen my regard for Jesus, if I gave those verses their literal meaning. This does not mean that the writers of the Gospels were untruthful persons. They wrote in a mood of exaltation. From my youth upward, I learned the art of estimating the value of scriptures on the basis of their ethical teaching. Miracles, therefore, had no interest for me. The miracles said to have been performed by Jesus, even if I had believed them literally, would not have reconciled me to any teaching that did not satisfy universal ethics. Somehow or other, words of religious teachers have for me, as I presume for millions, a living force which the same words uttered by ordinary mortals do not possess.

JESUS—A GREAT WORLD TEACHER

Jesus, then, to me is a great world teacher among others. He was to the devotees of his generation no doubt "the only begotten son of God." Their belief need not be mine. He affects my life no less because I regard him as one among the many begotten sons of God. The adjective "begotten" has, for me, a deeper and possibly a grander meaning than its literal meaning. For me, it implies spiritual birth. In his own times, he was the nearest to God.

Jesus atoned for the sins of those who accepted his teachings by being an infallible example to them. But the example was worth nothing to those who never troubled to change their lives. A regenerate outgrows the original taint, even as purified gold outgrows the original alloy.

I have made the frankest admission of my many sins. But I do not their burden on my shoulders. If I am journeying godward, as I feel I am, it is safe with me, for I feel the warmth of the sunshine of His presence. My austerities, fastings, and prayers are, I know, of no value, if I rely upon them for reforming me. But they have an inestimable value, if they represent, as I hope they do, the yearnings of a soul striving to lay his weary head in the lap of his Maker.

CHILDREN OF THE SAME GOD

The Gita has become for me the key to the scriptures of the world. It unravels for me the deepest mysteries to be found in them. I regard them with the same reverence that I pay to the Hindu scriptures. Hindus, Mussalmans, Christians, Parsis, Jews are convenient labels. But when I tear them down, I do not know which is which. We are all children of the same God. "Verily, verily, I say unto you, not every one that sayeth unto me 'Lord, Lord,' shall enter the Kingdom of Heaven, but he that doeth the will of my Father which is in Heaven shall enter the Kingdom" was said, though in different words, by all the great teachers of the world.

Harijan, April 18, 1936

WHY I AM NOT A CONVERT TO CHRISTIANITY

There is nothing in the world that would keep me from professing Christianity or any other faith, the moment I feel the truth of and the need for it. Where there is fear there is no religion. . . . If I could call myself, say, a Christian, or a Mussalman, with my own interpretation of the Bible or the Koran I should not hesitate to call myself either. For then Hindu, Christian and Mussalman would be synonymous terms.

Young India, September 2, 1926

An English friend has been at me for the past thirty years, trying to persuade me that there is nothing but damnation in Hinduism and that I must accept Christianity. When I was in jail I got, from separate sources, no less than three copies of *The Life of Sister Therese*, in the hope that I should follow her example and accept Jesus as the only begotten son of God and my Savior. I read the book prayerfully, but I could not accept even St. Therese's testimony for myself. I must say that I have an open mind, if indeed at this stage and age of my life I can be said to have an open mind on this question. Anyway, I claim to have an open mind in this sense that, if things were to happen to me as they did to Saul before he became Paul, I should not hesitate to be converted.

But today I rebel against orthodox Christianity, as I am convinced that it has distorted the message of Jesus. He was an Asiatic whose message was delivered through many media, and when it had the backing of a

Roman Emperor it became an imperialist faith as it remains to this day.

Harijan, May 30, 1936

Though I cannot claim to be a Christian in the sectarian sense, the example of Jesus' suffering is a factor in the composition of my undying faith in nonviolence which rules all my actions, worldly and temporal.

Harijan, January 7, 1939

ONLY BEGOTTEN SON OF GOD?

Gandhi: I regard Jesus as a great teacher of humanity, but I do not regard him as the only begotten son of God. That epithet in its material interpretation is quite unacceptable. Metaphorically we are all begotten sons of God, but for each of us there may be different begotten sons of God in a special sense ...

Question: But don't you believe in the perfection *of human nature, and don't you believe that Jesus had attained perfection?*

Gandhi: I believe in the *perfectibility* of human nature. Jesus came as near to perfection as possible. To say that he was perfect is to deny God's superiority to man. And then in this matter I have a theory of my own. Being necessarily limited by the bonds of flesh, we can attain perfection only after dissolution of the body. Therefore God alone is absolutely perfect. When He descends to earth, He of His own accord limits Himself. Jesus died on the Cross because he was limited by the flesh.

I do not need either the prophesies or the miracles to establish Jesus' greatness as a teacher. *Nothing can be more miraculous than the three years of his ministry.* There is no miracle in the story of the multitude being fed on a handful of loaves. A magician can create that illusion. But woe worth the day on which a magician would be hailed as the savior of humanity. As for Jesus raising the dead to life, well I doubt if the men he raised were really dead. I raised a relative's child from supposed death to life, but that was because the child was not dead, and but for my presence there she might have been cremated. But I saw that life was not extinct. I gave her an enema and she was restored to life. There was no miracle about it. I do not deny that Jesus had certain psychic powers and he was undoubtedly filled with the love of humanity. But he brought to life not people who were dead but who were believed to be dead. The laws of Nature are changeless, unchangeable, and there are no miracles in the sense of infringement or interruption of Nature's laws. But we limited beings fancy all kinds of things and impute our limitations to God. We may copy God, but not He us. We may not divide Time for Him; Time for Him is eternity. For us there is past, present, and future. And what is human life of a hundred years but less than a mere speck in the eternity of Time?

Harijan, April 17, 1937

WHAT JESUS MEANS TO ME

Although I have devoted a large part of my life to the study of religion and to discussion with religious leaders of all faiths, I know very well that I cannot but seem presumptuous in writing about Jesus Christ and trying to explain what He means to me. I do so only because my Christian friends have told me on more than a few occasions that for the very reason that I am not a Christian and that (I shall quote their words exactly) "I do not accept Christ in the bottom of my heart as the only Son of God," it is impossible for me to understand the profound significance of His teachings, or to know and interpret the greatest source of spiritual strength that man has ever known.

Although this may or may not be true in my case, I have reasons to believe that it is an erroneous point of view. I believe that such an estimate is incompatible with the message that Jesus Christ gave to the world. For He was, certainly, the highest example of One who wished to give everything, asking nothing in return, and not caring what creed might happen to be professed by the recipient. I am sure that if He were living here now among men, He would bless the lives of many who perhaps have never even heard His name, if only their lives embodied the virtues of which He was a living example on earth; the virtues of loving one's neighbor as oneself and of doing good and charitable works among one's fellow men.

What, then, does Jesus mean to me? To me, He was one of the greatest teachers humanity has ever had. To His believers, He was God's only begotten son. Could the fact that I do or do not accept this belief make Jesus have any more or less influence in my life? Is all the grandeur of His teaching and of His doctrine to be forbidden to me? I cannot believe so. To me it implies a spiritual birth. My interpretation, in other words, is that in Jesus' own life is the key of His nearness to God; that He expressed, as no other could, the spirit and will of God. It is in this sense that I see Him and recognize Him as the son of God. But I do believe that something of this spirit that Jesus exemplified in the highest measure, in its most profound human sense, does exist. I must believe this; if I did not believe it I should be a sceptic; and to be a sceptic is to live a life that is empty and lacks moral content. Or, what is the same thing, to condemn the entire human race to a negative end.

It is true that there certainly is reason for scepticism when one observes the bloody butchery that European aggressors have unloosed, and when one thinks about the misery and suffering prevalent in every corner of the world, as well as the pestilence and famine that always follow, terribly and inevitably, upon war. In the face of this, how can one speak seriously of the divine spirit incarnate in man? Because these acts of terror and murder offend the conscience of man; because man knows that they represent evil; because in the inner depths of his heart and of his mind, he deplores them.

And because, moreover, when he does not go astray, misled by false teachings or corrupted by false leaders, man has within his breast an impulse for good and a compassion that is the spark of divinity, and which some day, I believe, will burst forth into the full flower that is the hope of all mankind. An example of this flowering may be found in the figure and in the life of Jesus. I refuse to believe that there now exists or has ever existed a person that has not made use of His example to lessen his sins, even though he may have done so without realizing it. The lives of all have, in some greater or lesser degree, been changed by His presence, His actions, and the words spoken by His divine voice.

I believe that it is impossible to estimate the merits of the various religions of the world, and moreover I believe that it is unnecessary and harmful even to attempt it. But each one of them, in my judgment, embodies a common motivating force: the desire to uplift man's life and give it purpose. And because the life of Jesus has the significance and the transcendency to which I have alluded I believe that He belongs not solely to Christianity, but to the entire world; to all races and people, it matters little under what flag, name, or doctrine they may work, profess a faith, or worship a God inherited from their ancestors.

The Modern Review, October 1941

CHRIST—A PRINCE AMONGST SATYAGRAHIS

Buddha fearlessly carried the war into the enemy's camp and brought down on its knees an arrogant priesthood. Christ drove out the money-changers from the temple of Jerusalem and drew down curses from Heaven upon the hypocrites and the Pharisees. Both were for intensely direct action. But even as Buddha and Christ chastised they showed unmistakable gentleness and love behind every act of theirs. They would not raise a finger against their enemies, but would gladly surrender themselves rather than the truth for which they lived. Buddha would have died resisting the priesthood, if the majesty of his love had not proved to be equal to the task of bending the priesthood. Christ died on the Cross with a crown of thorns on his head defying the might of a whole empire. And if I raise resistance of a nonviolent character, I simply and humbly follow in the footsteps of the great teachers.

Young India, May 12, 1920

My reading of [the Bible] has clearly confirmed the opinion derived from a reading of the Hindu scriptures. Jesus mixed with the publicans and the sinners neither as dependent nor as a patron. He mixed with them to serve and to convert them to a life of truthfulness and purity. But he wiped the dust off his feet of those places which did not listen to his word. I hold it to be my duty not to countenance a son who disgraces himself by a life of shame and vice. Enlightened noncooperation is the expression of anguished love. . . . Would Jesus have accepted gifts from moneychangers, taken from them scholarships for his friends, and advanced loans to them to ply their nefarious traffic? Was his denunciation of hypocrites, Pharisees, and Sadducees merely in word? Or did he not actually invite the people to beware of them and shun them?

Young India, January 19, 1921

Chance threw Rome in my way. And I was able to see something of that great and ancient city and Mussolini, the unquestioned dictator of Italy. And what would not I have given to be able to bow my head before the living image at the Vatican of Christ Crucified. It was not without a wrench that I could tear myself away from that scene of living tragedy. I saw there at once that nations, like individuals, could only be made through the agony of the Cross and in no other way. Joy comes not out of infliction of pain on others, but out of pain voluntarily borne by onself.

Young India, December 31, 1931

The virtues of mercy, nonviolence, love and truth in any man can be truly tested only when they are pitted against ruthlessness, violence, hate and untruth.

If this is true, then it is incorrect to say that Ahimsa is of no avail before a murderer. It can certainly be said that to experiment with Ahimsa in face of a murderer is to seek self-destruction. But this is the real test of Ahimsa. He who gets himself killed out of sheer helplessness, however, can in nowise be said to have passed the test. He who when being kicked bears no anger against his murderer and even asks God to forgive him is truly nonviolent. History relates this of Jesus Christ.

With His dying breath on His Cross He is reported to have said: "Father, forgive them, for they know not what they do."

Harijan, April 28, 1946

The theory is that an adequate appeal to the heart never fails. Seeming failure is not of the law of Satyagraha but of incompetence of the satyagrahi by whatever cause induced. It may not be possible to give a complete historical instance. The name of Jesus at once comes to the lips. *It is an instance of brilliant failure.* And he has been acclaimed in the West as the prince of passive resisters. I showed years ago in South Africa that the adjective "passive" was a misnomer, at least as applied to Jesus. He was the most active resister known perhaps to history. His was nonviolence *par excellence.*

Harijan, June 30, 1946

Europe mistook the bold and brave resistance, full of wisdom, by Jesus of Nazareth for passive resistance, as if it was of the weak. As I read the New Testament for the first time, I detected no passivity, no weakness about Jesus as depicted in the four Gospels, and the meaning became clearer to me when I read Tolstoy's *Harmony of the Gospels* and his other kindred writings. Has not the West paid heavily in regarding Jesus as a passive resister? Christendom has been responsible for the wars which put to shame even those described in the Old Testament and other records, historical or semi-historical.

Harijan, December 7, 1947

── Chapter Three ──

Mission and Missionaries

APPEAL TO CHRISTIAN MISSIONARIES

The following is taken from an address to the Missionary Conference in Madras, on February 14, 1916.

Hinduism has become a conservative religion and, therefore, a mighty force. It is the most tolerant because it is non-proselytizing, and it is capable of expansion today as it has been found to be in the past. A Hindu refuses to change his religion, not necessarily because he considers it to be the best, but because he knows that he can complement it by introducing reforms. And what I have said about Hinduism is, I suppose, true of the other great faiths of the world, only it is held that it is specially so in the case of Hinduism.

If there is any substance in what I have said, will not the great missionary bodies of India, to whom she owes a deep debt of gratitude for what they have done and are doing, do still better and serve the spirit of Christianity better by dropping the goal of proselytizing while continuing their philanthropic work? I hope you will not consider this to be an impertinence on my part. I make the suggestion in all sincerity and with due humility. Moreover, I have some claim upon your attention.

I have endeavored to study the Bible. I consider it as part of my scriptures. The spirit of the Sermon on the Mount competes almost on equal terms with the *Bhagavad Gita* for the domination of my heart. I yield to no Christian in the strength of devotion with which I sing "Lead Kindly Light" and several other inspired hymns of a similar nature. I have come under the influence of noted Christian missionaries belonging to different denominations. And I enjoy to this day the privilege of friendship with some of them. You will perhaps, therefore, allow that I have offered the above suggestion not as a biased Hindu, but as an humble and impartial student of religion with great leanings toward Christianity. May it not be that the "Go ye unto all the world" message has been somewhat narrowly inter-

31

preted and the spirit of it missed? It will not be denied, I speak from experience, that many of the conversions are only so-called. In some cases, the appeal has gone not to the heart but to the stomach. And, in every case, a conversion leaves a sore behind it which, I venture to think, is avoidable.

Quoting again from experience, a new birth, a change of heart is perfectly possible in every one of the great faiths. I know I am now treading upon thin ice. But I do not apologize for saying that the frightful outrage that is just going on in Europe perhaps shows that the message of Jesus of Nazareth, the Son of Peace, has been little understood in Europe, and that light upon it may have to be thrown from the East.

Speeches & Writings of M. K. Gandhi, pp. 242-44

WESTERN CHRISTIANITY TODAY

It is my firm opinion that Europe today represents not the spirit of God or Christianity *but the spirit of Satan*. And Satan's successes are the greatest when he appears with the name of God on his lips. Europe is today only nominally Christian. It is really worshipping Mammon. "It is easier for a camel to pass through the eye of a needle than for a rich man to enter the Kingdom." Thus really spoke Jesus Christ. His so-called followers measure their moral progress by their material possessions.

The very national anthem of England is anti-Christian. Jesus, who asked his followers to love their enemies even as themselves, could not have sung of his enemies, "Confound his enemies, frustrate their knavish tricks."

Young India, September 8, 1920

I consider Western Christianity in its practical working a negation of Christ's Christianity. I cannot conceive Jesus, if he was living in the flesh in our midst, approving of modern Christian organization, public worship, or modern ministry. If Indian Christians will simply cling to the Sermon on the Mount, which was delivered not merely to the peaceful disciples but a groaning world, they would not go wrong, and they would find that no religion is false; and that if all live according to their lights and in the fear of God, they would not need to worry about organizations, forms of worship, and ministry. The Pharisees had all that, but Jesus would have none of it, for they were using their office as a cloak for hypocrisy and worse. Cooperation with forces of Good and non-cooperation with forces of Evil are the two things we need for a good and pure life, whether it is called Hindu, Muslim, or Christian.

Young India, September 27, 1921

HOW TO SERVE CHRIST BETTER

The following is taken from a conversation with missionaries in Bengal, recorded by Gandhi's secretary, Mahadev Desai. One of the missionaries asked Gandhi to tell them "how to serve Christ better."

"Proselytizing [Gandhi said] has done some good, but it has perhaps been outweighed by the evil it has left behind. Whether you profess one religion or another is of no consequence whatsoever. What God will say, and wants us to say, is not what we profess with our lips but what we believe in our hearts; and there is no shadow of doubt that there are thousands and thousands of men and women in the world who do not know the Bible or the name of Jesus or of His amazing sacrifice, but who are far more God-fearing than many a Christian who knows the Bible, offers his prayers regularly, and believes sincerely that he follows all the Commandments. Religion is made of sterner stuff, and it is impossible for us frail, weak human beings to understand what people mean when they say that they would be better if they professed something else from what they did."

[Gandhi] recalled his conversation with a South African chaplain who, after considerable questioning and cross-questioning, had told him that he would not thenceforth want to convert him. *"It is not he who says 'Lord, Lord,'* I told him, *who enters the Kingdom of Heaven, but he that doeth His will.* I reminded him, 'I am conscious of my weaknesses, and try to fight them—not in my own strength but in the strength of God. Is that enough or do you wish me to repeat parrot-like that Jesus has cleansed me from all sin?' He stopped me and said, 'I understand what you mean.' So I say that instead of wanting to find out how many heads you count as Christian, work away like . . . silently among the people and let your work be the silent testimony of your worth. What do you want to convert them for? If your contact with them ennobles them, makes them forget untruth and all evil and brings them a ray of light, is that not enough? Or in case you have taken charge of an orphan, if you feed him and clothe him, is that not enough? Is that not its own reward? Or must you have a mechanical confession from him that he is a Christian?

"We see today a rivalry, a war going on among different religions as to the number of adherents each can boast. I feel deeply humiliated and feel that in every one of the feats we claim to have performed in converting people to our faith we are denying our God and being untrue to ourselves."

In the latter part of his speech, he explained that if missionaries truly wanted to serve Christ better they must pick up the poorest portion of humanity and identify themselves with them, never seeking protection from temporal power, but ever glorying in the strength of God.

Young India, June 18, 1925

AN ADDRESS TO MISSIONARIES

Not many of you perhaps know that my association with Christians— not Christians so-called, but real Christians—dates from 1889 when as a lad I found myself in London; and that association has grown riper as years have rolled on. In South Africa where I found myself in the midst of inhospitable surroundings I was able to make hundreds of Christian friends. . . .

My acquaintance, therefore, this evening with so many missionaries is by no means a new thing. There was even a time in my life when a very sincere and intimate friend of mine, a great and good Quaker, had designs on me [laughter]. He thought that I was too good not to become a Christian. I was sorry to have disappointed him. One missionary friend of mine in South Africa still writes to me and asks me, "How is it with you?" I have always told this friend that so far as I know it is all well with me. If it was prayer that these friends expected me to make, I was able to tell them that every day the heart-felt prayer within the closed door of my closet went to the Almighty to show me light and give wisdom and courage to follow that light.

In answer to promises made to one of these Christian friends of mine I thought it my duty to see one of the biggest of Indian Christians, as I was told he was—the late Kali Charan Banerjee.* I went over to him—I am telling you of the deep search that I have undergone in order that I might leave no stone unturned to find out the true path—I went to him with an absolutely open mind and in a receptive mood, and I met him also under circumstances which were most affecting. I found that there was much in common between Mr. Banerjee and myself. His simplicity, his humility, his courage, his truthfulness, all these things I have all along admired. He met me when his wife was on her deathbed. You cannot imagine a more impressive scene, a more ennobling circumstance. I told Mr. Banerjee, "I have come to you as a seeker"—this was in 1901—"I have come to you in fulfillment of a sacred promise I have made to some of my dearest Christian friends that I will leave no stone unturned to find out the true light." I told him that I had given my friends the assurance that no worldly gain would keep me away from the light, if I could but see it. Well, I am not going to engage you in giving a description of the little discussion that we had between us. It was very good, very noble. I came away, not sorry, not dejected, not disappointed, but I felt sad that even Mr. Banerjee could not convince me. This was my final deliberate striving to realize Christianity as it was presented to me.

Today my position is that, though I admire much in Christianity, I am unable to identify myself with orthodox Christianity. I must tell you in all humility that Hinduism, as I know it, entirely satisfies my soul, fills my whole being, and I find a solace in the Bhagavadgita and Upanishads that I miss even in the Sermon on the Mount. Not that I do not prize the ideal presented therein, not that some of the precious teachings in the Sermon on the Mount have not left a deep impression upon me, but I must confess to you that when doubts haunt me, when disappointments stare me in the face, and when I see not one ray of light on the horizon I turn to the

---

* Kali Charan Banerjee was a prominent Christian Congressman.

Bhagavadgita and find a verse to comfort me; and I immediately begin to smile in the midst of overwhelming sorrow. My life has been full of external tragedies and, if they have not left any visible and indelible effect on me, I owe it to the teaching of the Bhagavadgita.

I have told you all these things in order to make it absolutely clear to you where I stand, so that I may have, if you will, closer touch with you. I must add that I did not stop at studying the Bible and the commentaries and other books on Christianity that my friends place in my hands; but I said to myself, if I was to find my satisfaction through reasoning, I must study the scriptures of other religions also and make my choice. And I turned to the Koran. I tried to understand what I could of Judaism as distinguished from Christianity. I studied Zoroastrianism and I came to the conclusion that all religions were right but every one of them was imperfect, imperfect naturally and necessarily, because they were interpreted with our poor intellects, sometimes with our poor hearts, and more often misinterpreted. In all religions I found to my grief that there were various and even contradictory interpretations of some texts, and I said to myself, "Not these things for me. If I want the satisfaction of my soul, I must feel my way. I must wait silently upon God and ask Him to guide me." There is a beautiful verse in Sanskrit which says, "God helps only when man feels utterly helpless and utterly humble." Some of you have come from the Tamil land. When I was studying Tamil, I found in one of the books of Dr. Pope a Tamil proverb which means "God helps the helpless." I have given you this life story of my own experience for you to ponder over.

You, the missionaries, come to India thinking that you come to a land of heathens, of idolaters, of men who do not know God. One of the greatest of Christian divines, Bishop Heber, wrote the two lines which have always left a sting with me: "Where every prospect pleases, and only man is vile." I wish he had not written them. My own experience in my travels throughout India has been to the contrary. I have gone from one end of the country to the other, without any prejudice, in a relentless search after truth, and I am not able to say that here in this fair land, watered by the great Ganges, the Brahmaputra and the Jumna, man is vile. He is not vile. He is as much a seeker after truth as you and I are, possibly more so.

This reminds me of a French book translated for me by a French friend. It is an account of an imaginary expedition in search of knowledge. One party landed in India and found Truth and God personified, in a little Pariah's hut. I tell you there are many such huts belonging to the untouchables where you will certainly find God. They do not reason, but they persist in their belief that God is. They depend upon God for His assistance and find it too. There are many stories told throughout the length and breadth of India about these noble untouchables. Vile as some of them may be there are the noblest specimens of humanity in their midst.

But does my experience exhaust itself merely with the untouchables? No, I am here to tell you that there are non-Brahmins, there are Brahmins who are as fine specimens of humanity as you will find in any place on the earth. There are Brahmins today in India who are embodiments of self-sacrifice, godliness, and humility. There are Brahmins who are devoting themselves body and soul to the service of untouchables, with no expectation of reward from the untouchables, but with execration from orthodoxy. They do not mind it, because in serving Pariahs they are serving God. I can quote chapter and verse from my experience.

I place these facts before you in all humility for the simple reason that you may know this land better, the land to which you have come to serve. You are here to find out the distress of the people of India and remove it. But I hope you are here also in a receptive mood, and if there is anything that India has to give, you will not stop your ears, you will not close your eyes, and steel your hearts, but open up your ears, eyes, and most of all your hearts to receive all that may be good in this land. I give you my assurance that there is a great deal of good in India. Do not flatter yourselves with the belief that a mere recital of that celebrated verse in St. John n..kes a man a Christian. If I have read the Bible correctly, I know many men who have never heard the name of Jesus Christ or have even rejected the official interpretation of Christianity who will, probably, if Jesus came in our midst today in the flesh, be owned by him more than many of us. I therefore ask you to approach the problem before you with openheartedness and humility.

I was engaged in a friendly conversation with some missionaries this morning. I do not want to relate that conversation. But I do want to say that they are fine specimens of humanity. They did not want to misunderstand me, but I had to pass nearly one hour and a half in my attempt to explain to them that in writing what I had written I had not written anything in a spirit of ill-will or hatred towards Englishmen. I was hard put to it to carry that conviction. In fact I do not know whether I carried that conviction to them at all. If salt loseth its savor, wherewith shall it be salted? If I could not drive home the truth that was in me to the three friends who certainly came with open minds, how should I fare with others?

It has often occurred to me that a seeker after truth has to be silent. I know the wonderful efficacy of silence. I visited a Trappist monastery in South Africa. A beautiful place it was. Most of the inmates of that place were under a vow of silence. I enquired of the Father the motive of it, and he said that the motive was apparent. "We are frail human beings. We do not know very often what to say. If we want to listen to the still small voice that is always speaking within us, it will not be heard if we continually speak." I understood that precious lesson. I know the secret of silence. I do not know just now as I speak to you whether it would not have been wise if I had said nothing to those friends beyond saying, "We shall know each other better when the mists have rolled away." As I speak to you, I feel humiliated. Why did I argue with these friends? But I say these things to you first of all to make this confession, and secondly to tell you also that, if you will refuse to see the other side, if you will refuse to understand what India is thinking, then you will deny yourselves the real privilege of service.

I have told my missionary friends, "Noble as you are, you have isolated yourselves from the people whom you want to serve." I cannot help recalling to you the conversation I related in Darjeeling at the Missionary Language School. Lord Salisbury* was waited upon by a deputation of missionaries in connection with China and this deputation wanted protection. I cannot recall the exact words but give you the purport of the answer Lord Salisbury gave. He said, "Gentlemen, if you want to go to China to preach the message of Christianity, then do not ask for assistance of the temporal power. Go with your lives in your hands and, if the people of China want to kill you, imagine that you have been killed in the service of God." Lord Salisbury was right. Christian missionaries come to India under the shadow, or, if you like, under the protection of a temporal power, and it creates an impassable bar.

If you give me statistics that so many orphans have been reclaimed and brought to the Christian faith, I would accept them but I do not feel convinced thereby that it is your mission. In my opinion your mission is infinitely superior to that. You want to find men in India and, if you want to do that, you will have to go to the lowly cottages — not to give them something, but maybe to take something from them. A true friend as I claim to be of the missionaries of India and of the Europeans, I speak to you what I feel from the bottom of my heart. I miss receptiveness, humility, willingness on your part to identify yourselves with the masses of India. I have talked straight from my heart. May it find a response from your hearts.

QUESTIONS:

How do you think the missionaries should identify themselves with the masses?

Gandhi: The question is somewhat embarrassing. But I would venture to say, "Copy Charlie Andrews."

What definite work would you suggest that a missionary should do for and among the masses?

Gandhi: Since I have been challenged I must unhesitatingly answer, "The spinning wheel."** You naturally laugh, but if you knew the masses as I do, you will look upon this very simple instrument of torture (takli) with

* Lord Salisbury, the British prime minister.
** The spinning wheel, or *charka*, was the Gandhian symbol of *swadeshi*, or self-reliance. The British colonial economy forced India to exchange cotton for British fabric, thus undermining the local economy and fostering economic dependence. In response Gandhi embraced the spinning wheel and the production of homespun "khadi," which provided employment for the masses, affirmed the dignity of labor, and offered a form of real economic resistance to colonialism.

seriousness. You cannot present the hungry and famished masses with God. Their God is their food. General Booth* knew what he was doing when at his numerous depots the first thing he did to the hungry men and women who flocked there was to give them a plate of soup. Before he would give them their next meal he called upon them to make splinters for his match factory and then he introduced them to God. The famished millions are famishing not because there is not enough food produced in India but because they have no work to do. The only work for the millions is the spinning wheel. I know the Industrial Mission House in Calcutta. It is good in its way, but it does not touch even the fringe of the question. The problem is how to take work to the cottages of these men, cottages which are scattered over a surface 1900 miles long and 1500 broad. They will not take the spinning wheel unless they learn the art themselves and unless they spin to set an example to these men who have lost faith in themselves and faith in everything and everybody. And the spinning wheel is useless unless you and I wear *khadi*. Hence it is that I have not hesitated to say to Lord Reading or to Lord Willingdon** that I will not be satisfied unless they and their orderlies are dressed from top to toe in *khadi*.

Do you definitely feel the presence of the living Christ within you?
Gandhi: If it is the historical Jesus surnamed Christ that you refer to, I must say I do not. If it is an adjective signifying one of the names of God, then I must say I do feel the presence of God—call Him Christ, call Him Krishna, call Him Rama. We have one thousand names to denote God, and if I did not feel the presence of God within me, I see so much of misery and disappointment every day that I would be a raving maniac and my destination would be the Hooghli [River].

Young India, August 6, 1925

FOR CHRISTIAN INDIANS

When I was a youth, I remember a Hindu having become a convert to Christianity. The whole town understood that the initiation took the shape of this well-bred Hindu partaking of beef and brandy in the name of Jesus Christ, and discarding his national costume. I learned in later years that such a convert, as so many of my missionary friends put it, came to a life of freedom out of a life of bondage, to a life of plenty out of one of penury. As I wander about throughout the length and breadth of India, I see many Christian Indians almost ashamed of their birth, certainly of their ancestral religion, and of their ancestral dress. The aping of Europeans on the part of Anglo-Indians is bad enough, but the aping of them by Indian converts

---

* William Booth, founder of the Salvation Army.
** Lord Reading and Lord Willingdon—respectively Viceroy and Presidency Governor of India. Willingdon later became Viceroy as well.

is a violence done to their country and shall I say, even to their new religion. There is a verse in the New Testament to bid Christians avoid meat, if it would offend their neighbors. Meat here, I presume, includes drink and dress. I can appreciate uncompromising avoidance of all that is evil in the old, but where there is not only question of anything evil but where an ancient practice may be even desirable, it would be a crime to part with it when one knows for certain that the giving up would deeply hurt relatives and friends.

WHAT CONVERSION SHOULD MEAN

Conversion must not mean denationalization. Conversion should mean a definite giving up of the evil of the old, adoption of all the good of the new and a scrupulous avoidance of everything evil in the new. Conversion, therefore, should mean a life of greater dedication to one's own country, greater surrender to God, greater self-purification.

Years ago, I met the late Kali Charan Bannerjee. Had I not known before I went there that he was a Christian, I should certainly not have noticed from the outward appearance of his home that he was one. It was no different from an ordinary modern Hindu home—simple and meager in furniture. The great man was dressed like an ordinary un-Europeanized Hindu Bengali. I know that there is a marvelous change coming over Christian Indians. There is on the part of a large number of them a longing to revert to original simplicity, a longing to belong to the nation and to serve it, but the process is too slow. There need be no waiting. It requires not much effort. The late Principal Rudra* and I used often to discuss this evil tendency. I well remember how he used to deplore it. I am offering a tribute to the memory of a dead friend when I inform the reader that he used often to express his grief that it was too late in life for him to change some of the unnecessary European habits to which he was brought up.

Is it not truly deplorable that many Christian Indians discard their own mother tongue, bring up their children only to speak in English? Do they not thereby completely cut themselves adrift from the nation in whose midst they have to live? But they may answer in self-defense that many Hindus, and even Mussalmans, have become denationalized. The *Tu Quoque* argument serves no useful purpose. I am writing not as a critic but as a friend who has enjoyed the closest intimacy with hundreds of Christian Indians. I want my missionary friends and Christian Indians to reciprocate the spirit in which these lines are written. I write in the name and for the sake of heart unity which I want to see established among the people of this land professing different faiths. In Nature, there is a fundamental unity running through all the diversity we see about us. Religions are no exception to the

---

* Susil Kumar Rudra was the first Indian Principal of St. Stephen's College in Delhi. A devout Christian, he was distinguished, in Gandhi's eyes, for his appreciation of other faiths.

natural law. They are given to mankind so as to accelerate the process of realization of fundamental unity.

Young India, August 20, 1925

DIRECT AND INDIRECT CONTRIBUTION OF MISSIONARIES

I would like to know your very frank evaluation of the work of Christian missionaries in India. Do you believe that Christianity has some contribution to make to the life of our country? Can we do without Christianity?

Gandhi: In my opinion Christian missionaries have done good to us indirectly. Their direct contribution is probably more harmful than otherwise. I am against the modern method of proselytizing. Years' experience of proselytizing both in South Africa and India has convinced me that it has not raised the general moral tone of the converts who have imbibed the superficialities of European civilization, and have missed the teaching of Jesus. I must be understood to refer to the general tendency and not to brilliant exceptions. The indirect contribution, on the other hand, of Christian missionary effort is great. It has stimulated Hindus and Mussalmans in religious research. It has forced us to put our own houses in order. I also count, amongst indirect results, the great educational and curative institutions of Christian missions, because they have been established, not for their own sakes, but as an aid to proselytizing.

The world, and therefore we, can no more do without the teachings of Jesus than we can without that of Mohammed or the Upanishads. I hold all these to be complementary of one another, in no case exclusive. Their true meaning, their interdependence and interrelation, have still to be revealed to us. We are but indifferent representatives of our respective faiths, which we belie more often than not.

Young India, December 17, 1925

May we know what form, in your opinion, missionary work should take if the missionaries are to stay in India?

Gandhi: Yes, They have to alter their attitude. Today, they tell people that there is no salvation for them except through the Bible and through *Christianity*. It is customary to decry other religions and to offer their own as the only one that can bring deliverance. That attitude should be radically changed. Let them appear before the people as they are, and try to rejoice in seeing Hindus become better Hindus and Mussalmans better Mussalmans. Let them start work at the bottom, let them enter into what is best in their life and offer nothing inconsistent with it. That will make their work far more efficacious, and what they will say and offer to the people will be appreciated without suspicion and hostility. In a word, let them go to the people not as patrons, but as one of them, not to oblige them but to serve them and to work among them.

Young India, July 14, 1927

REREAD THE MESSAGE OF THE BIBLE

From "Talks with Missionaries," an article by Mahadev Desai.

Gandhiji opened the discussion by claiming himself to be a friend of the missionaries, ever since his close contact with them in South Africa. "Though I have been a friend, I have always been a critic, not from any desire to be critical, but because I have felt that I would be a better friend if I opened out my heart, even at the risk of wounding their feelings. They never allowed me to think that they felt hurt, they certainly never resented my criticism." Then he referred to his first speech before the missionaries in India on Swadeshi, since which twelve years had rolled away and with them much of the mists also.

"The first distinction I would like to make, after these prefatory remarks, between your missionary work and mine, is that while I am strengthening the faith of the people, you are undermining it. Your work, I have always held, will be all the richer if you accept as settled facts the faiths of the people you come to serve—faiths which, however crude, are valuable to them. And in order to appreciate what I say, it becomes perhaps necessary to reread the message of the Bible in terms of what is happening around us. The word is the same, but the spirit ever broadens intensively and extensively, and it might be that many things in the Bible will have to be reinterpreted in the light of discoveries—not of modern science, but in the spiritual world in the shape of direct experiences common to all faiths. The fundamental verses of St. John do require to be reread and reinterpreted. I have come to feel that, like us human beings, words have their evolution from stage to stage in the contents they hold. For instance the contents of the richest word—God—are not the same to every one of us. They will vary with the experience of each. They will mean one thing to the Santhal and another to his next-door neighbor Rabindranath Tagore. But God himself is a long-suffering God who puts up with any amount of abuse and misinterpretation. If we were to put the spiritual experiences together, we would find a resultant which would answer the cravings of human nature. Christianity is 1900 years old, Islam is 1300 years old; who knows the possibility of either? I have not read the Vedas in the original, but have tried to assimilate their spirit and have not hesitated to say that, though the Vedas may be 13,000 years old—or even a million years old, as they well may be, for the word of God is as old as God Himself—even the Vedas must be interpreted in the light of our experience. The powers of God should not be limited by the limitations of our understanding. To you who have come to teach India, I therefore say, you cannot give without taking. If you have come to give rich treasures of experiences, open your hearts out to receive the treasures of this land, and you will not be disappointed, neither will you have misread the message of the Bible."

QUESTIONS

What then are we doing? Are we doing the right thing?

Gandhi: You are trying to do the right thing in the wrong way. I want you to complement the faith of the people instead of undermining it. I would say to you, make us better Hindus, i.e., better men or women. Why should a man, even if he becomes a Christian, be torn from his surroundings? Whilst a boy I heard it being said that to become a Christian was to have a brandy bottle in one hand and beef in the other. Things are better now, but it is not unusual to find Christianity synonymous with denationalization and Europeanization. Must we give up our simplicity to become better people? Do not lay the axe at our simplicity.

There are not only two issues before us, viz., to serve and to teach; there is a third issue, viz., evangelizing, declaring the glad tidings of the coming of Jesus and his death in redemption for our sins. What is the right way of giving the good news? We need not undermine the faith, but we may make people lose their faith in lesser things.

Gandhi: That leads me into the region of interpretation. Whilst I must not enter into it, I may suggest that God did not bear the Cross only 1900 years ago, but He bears it today. It would be poor comfort to the world if it had to depend upon a historical God who died 2,000 years ago. Do not then preach the God of history, but show Him as He lives today through you. In South Africa I met a number of friends, and read a number of books . . . all giving their own interpretations, and I said to myself I must not bother myself with these conflicting interpretations. It is better to allow our lives to speak for us than our words. C. F. Andrews never preaches. He is incessantly doing his work. He finds enough work and stays where he finds it and takes no credit for bearing the Cross. I have the honor to know hundreds of honest Christians, but I have not known one better than Andrews.

But what about animistic beliefs? Should they not be corrected?

Gandhi: Well, we have been working amongst the so-called untouchables and backward classes, and we have never bothered ourselves with their beliefs, animistic or otherwise. Superstitions and undesirable things go as soon as we begin to live the correct life. I concern myself not with their beliefs but with asking them to do the right thing. As soon as they do it, their belief rights itself.

How can we help condemning if we feel that our Christian truth is the only reality?

Gandhi: That brings me to the duty of tolerance. If you cannot feel that the other faith is as true as yours, you should feel at least that the men are as true as you. The intolerance of the Christian missionaries does not, I am glad to say, take the ugly shape it used to take some years ago. Think of the caricature of Hinduism, which one finds in so many publications of the Christian Literature Society. A lady wrote to me the other day saying that unless I embraced Christianity all my work would be worth nothing. And of course that Christianity must mean what she understands as such! Well, all I can say is that it is a wrong attitude.

Young India, August 11, 1927

FAITH HAS TO BE LIVED

Believing that Christ was a revelation of God, Christians of America have sent to India thousands of their sons and daughters to tell the people of India about Christ. Will you, in return, kindly give us your interpretation of Hinduism and make a comparison of Hinduism with the teachings of Christ?

Gandhi: I have ventured, at several missionary meetings, to tell English and American missionaries that if they could have refrained from "telling" India about Christ and had merely lived the life enjoined upon them by the Sermon on the Mount, India, instead of suspecting them, would have appreciated their living in the midst of her children and directly profited by their presence. Holding this view, I can "tell" American friends nothing about Hinduism by way of "return." I do not believe in people telling others of their faith, especially with a view to conversion. Faith does not admit of telling. It has to be lived and then it becomes self-propagating.

Young India, October 20, 1927

Confuse not *Jesus' teaching* with what passes as modern *civilization* and pray do not do unconscious violence to the people among whom you cast your lot. It is no part of that call, I assure you, to tear up the life of the people of the East by its roots. Tolerate whatever is good in them and do not hastily, with your preconceived notions, judge them. Do not judge lest you be judged yourselves.

In spite of your belief in the greatness of Western Civilization and in spite of your pride in all your achievements, I plead with you for humility, and ask you to leave some little room for doubt in which, as Tennyson sang, there was more truth—though by "doubt" he certainly meant a different thing. Let us each one live our life, and if ours is the right life, where is the cause for hurry? It will react of itself.

Young India, December 8, 1927

CONVERSION

What is the contribution of Christianity to the national life of India? I mean the influence of Christ as apart from Christianity, for, I am afraid, there is a wide gulf separating the two at present.

Gandhi: Aye, there lies the rub. It is not possible to consider the teaching of a religious teacher apart from the lives of his followers. Unfortunately, Christianity in India has been inextricably mixed up for the last one hundred and fifty years with the British rule. It appears to us as synonymous with materialistic civilization and imperialistic exploitation by the stronger white races of the weaker races of the world. Its contribution to India has been, therefore, largely of a negative character.

Do you disbelieve in all conversion?

Gandhi: I disbelieve in the conversion of one person by another. My effort should never be to undermine another's faith, but to make him a better follower of his own faith. This implies belief in the truth of all religions and, therefore, respect for them. It again implies true humility, a recognition of the fact that the Divine Light having been vouchsafed to all religions through an imperfect medium of flesh, they must share, in more or less degree, the imperfection of the vehicle.

Is it not our duty to help our fellow beings to the maximum of truth that we may possess, to share with them our deepest spiritual experiences?

Gandhi: I am sorry I must again differ from you, for the simple reason that the deepest spiritual truths are always unutterable. That Light, to which you refer, transcends speech. It can be felt only through the inner experience. And then the highest truth needs no communicating, for it is by its very nature self-propelling. It radiates its influence silently as the rose its fragrance without the intervention of a medium.

But even God sometimes speaks through His prophets.

Gandhi: Yes, but the prophets speak not through the tongue, but through their lives. I have, however, known that in this matter I am up against a solid wall of Christian opinion.

Oh, no. Even among Christians there is a school of thought—and it is growing—which holds that the authoritarian method should not be employed, but that each individual should be left to discover the deepest truths of life for himself. The argument advanced is that the process of spiritual discovery is bound to vary in the case of different individuals according to their varying needs and temperaments. In other words, they feel that propaganda, in the accepted sense of the term, is not the most effective method.

Gandhi: I am glad to hear you say this. That is what Hinduism certainly inculcates.

Young India, March 21, 1929

"PHYSICIAN, HEAL THYSELF"

I hold that proselytizing under the cloak of humanitarian work is, to say the least, unhealthy. It is most certainly resented by the people here. Religion, after all, is a deeply personal matter, it touches the heart. Why should I change my religion because a doctor who professes Christianity as his religion has cured me of some disease, or why should the doctor expect or suggest such a change whilst I am under his influence? Is not medical relief its own reward and satisfaction? Or why should I, whilst I am in a missionary educational institution, have Christian teaching thrust upon me? In my opinion, these practices are not uplifting and give rise to suspicion if not even secret hostility. The methods of conversion must be like Caesar's wife, above suspicion. Faith is not imparted like secular subjects. It is given through the language of the heart. If a man has a living faith in him, it spreads its aroma like the rose its scent. Because of its invisibility, the extent of its influence is far wider than that of the visible beauty of the color of the petals.

I am, then, not against conversion. But I am against the modern methods of it. Conversion nowadays has become a matter of business, like any other. I remember having read a missionary report saying how much it cost per head to convert and then presenting a budget for "the next harvest."

It follows from what I have said above that India is in no need of conversion of the kind I have in mind. Conversion, in the sense of self-purification, self-realization, is the crying need of the times. That, however, is not what is ever meant by proselytizing. To those who would convert India, might it not be said: "Physician, heal thyself!"

Young India, April 23, 1931

AROMA OF CHRISTIANITY

Has India benefited by Christianity?

Gandhi: Indirectly. The contacts of some of the noblest Christians could not but benefit us. We studied their lives, we came in contact with them, and they naturally ennobled us. But, as regards missionary activities as such, I cannot but use the language of caution. The very least I would say is that I doubt if they have benefited India. The most I could say is that they have repelled India from Christianity and placed a barrier between Christian life and Hindu or Mussalman life. When I go to your Scriptures I do not see the barrier raised, but when I see a missionary I find that barrier rising up before my eyes. I want you to accept this testimony from one who was for a time susceptible to those influences. The missionaries working in colleges and hospitals, too, have served us with the mental reservation that through the hospital and the college they want people to come to Christ. I have a definite feeling that if you want us to feel the aroma of Christianity, you must copy the rose. The rose irresistibly draws people to itself, and the scent remains with them. Even so, the aroma of Christianity is subtler even than that of the rose and should, therefore, be imparted in an even quieter and more imperceptible manner, if possible.

Young India, October 15, 1931

Why do you refuse to enter God's House, if Jesus invites you? Why does not India take up the Cross?

Gandhi: If Jesus has reference to God, I have never refused to enter the House of God; indeed, every moment I am trying to enter it. If Jesus represents not a person, but the principle of nonviolence, India has accepted its protecting power.

Young India, December 31, 1931

What is the most effective way of preaching the Gospel of Christ?

Gandhi: To live the Gospel is the most effective way—most effective in the beginning, in the middle, and in the end. Preaching jars on me and makes no appeal to me, and I get suspicious of missionaries who preach. But I love those who never preach, but live the life according to their lights. Their lives are silent yet most effective testimonies. Therefore, I cannot say what to preach, but I can say that a life of service and uttermost simplicity is the best preaching. If, therefore, you go on serving people and ask them also to serve, they would understand. But you quote instead John 3:16 and ask them to believe it. That has no appeal to me, and I am sure people will not understand it. Where there has been acceptance of the Gospel through preaching, my complaint is that there has been some motive.

But we also see it, and we try our best to guard against it.

Gandhi: But you can't guard against it. One sordid motive vitiates the whole preaching. It is like a drop of poison which fouls the whole food. Therefore, I should do without any preaching at all. A rose does not need to preach. It simply spreads its fragrance. The fragrance is its own sermon. If it had human understanding and if it could engage a number of preachers, the preachers would not be able to sell more roses than the fragrance itself could do. The fragrance of religious and spiritual life is much finer and subtler than that of the rose.

But we, Christians, feel that we, who have something to share, must share it with others. If we want consolation, we find it from the Bible. Now, as for the Harijans, who have no solace to get from Hinduism, how are we to meet their spiritual needs?

Gandhi: By behaving just like the rose. Does the rose proclaim itself, or is it self-propagated? Has it an army of missionaries proclaiming its beauties?

But supposing someone asked us: "When did you get the scent?"

Gandhi: The rose, if it had sense and speech, would say: "Fool, don't you see that I got it from my Maker?"

But if someone asks you: "Then is there no book?"

Gandhi: You will then say: "Yes, for me there is the Bible." If they were to ask me, I would present to some the Quran, to some the Gita, to some the Bible and to some Tulsidas' *Ramayana*. I am like a wise doctor prescribing what is necessary for each patient.

But I find difficulty in getting much from the Gita.
Gandhi: You may, but I do not find any difficulty in getting much from the Bible as well as from the Quran.

Harijan, March 29, 1935

THE WILL OF GOD

Last came the question of questions which missionary friends are not tired of asking and Gandhiji is not tired of answering: "You would prevent missionaries coming to India in order to baptize?"

"Who am I to prevent them? If I had power and could legislate, I should certainly stop all proselytizing. It is the cause of much avoidable conflict between classes and unnecessary heart-burning among missionaries. But I should welcome people of any nationality if they came to serve here for the sake of service. In Hindu households the advent of a missionary has meant the disruption of the family coming in the wake of change of dress, manners, language, food, and drink."

"Is it not the old conception you are referring to? No such thing is now associated with proselytization."

"The outward condition has perhaps changed, but the inward mostly remains. Vilification of Hindu religion, though subdued, is there. If there was a radical change in the missionaries' outlook would Murdoch's books be allowed to be sold in mission depots? Are those books prohibited by missionary societies? There is nothing but vilification of Hinduism in those books. You talk of the conception being no longer there. Only the other day a missionary descended on a famine area with money in his pocket, distributed it among the famine stricken, converted them to his fold, took charge of their temple, and demolished it. This is outrageous. The temple could not belong to the converted Hindus, and it could not belong to the Christian missionary. But this friend goes and gets it demolished at the hands of the very men who only a little while ago believed that God was there."

The visitor seemed to be touched. Perhaps she had not heard of the incident. She said, "In our hospital we do not try to influence our patients in their religious beliefs. Our doctor says we should not take an undue advantage of people in distress coming to us for treatment. But, Mr. Gandhi, why do you object to proselytization as such? Is not there enough in the Bible to authorize us to invite people to a better way of life?"

"Oh yes, but it does not mean that they should be made members of the Church. If you interpret your texts in the way you seem to do, you straightaway condemn a large part of humanity unless it believes as you do. If Jesus came to earth again, he would disown many things that are being done in the name of Christianity. It is not he who says 'Lord, Lord' that is a Christian, but 'He that doeth the will of the Lord' that is a true Christian. And cannot he who has not heard the name of Christ Jesus do the will of the Lord?"

Mahadev Desai in *Harijan*, May 11, 1935

"JUDGE NOT LEST YE BE JUDGED"

I believe that there is no such thing as conversion from one faith to another in the accepted sense of the term. It is a highly personal matter for the individual and his God. I may not have any design upon my neighbor as to his faith, which I must honor even as I honor my own. For I regard all the great religions of the world as true, at any rate for the people professing them, as mine is true for me. Having reverently studied the scriptures of the world, I have no difficulty in perceiving the beauties in all of them. I could no more think of asking a Christian or a Mussalman or a Parsi or a Jew to change his faith than I would think of changing my own. This makes me no more oblivious of the limitations of the professors of those faiths than it makes me of the grave limitations of the professors of mine. And seeing that it takes all my resources in trying to bring my practice to the level of my faith and in preaching the same to my coreligionists, I do not dream of preaching to the followers of other faiths. "Judge not lest ye be judged" is a sound maxim for one's conduct.

It is a conviction daily growing upon me that the great and rich Christian missions will render true service to India, if they can persuade themselves to confine other activities to the humanitarian service without ulterior motive of converting India or at least her unsophisticated villagers to Christianity, and destroying their social superstructure which, notwithstanding its many defects, has stood now from time immemorial the onslaughts upon it from within and from without. Whether they—the missionaries—and we wish it or not, what is true in the Hindu faith will abide, what is untrue will fall to pieces. Every living faith must have within itself the power of rejuvenation, if it is to live.

Harijan, September 28, 1935

A DISCOURSE WITH CHRISTIAN FRIENDS

Dr. Ceresole* walked one morning to Sevagram,** wading through ankle-deep mud, and had long talks with Gandhiji in his hut. He is a pilgrim to the Kingdom of Heaven, and he loves to compare notes when he meets a kindred spirit like Gandhiji.

* Pierre Ceresole was a prominent Swiss pacifist.
** Sevagram—Service Village, one of Gandhi's ashrams.

"Religion," he said, "which should bind us divides us. Is it not a sorry spectacle that, whilst people of various denominations find no difficulty in working together all day in hearty cooperation, they must disband when the time for prayer comes? Is religion then meant to divide us? Must it be allowed to become an expression of conceit rather than of a desire to be of service?"

Dr. Ceresole thus did some loud thinking when he went to Sevagram one morning with two missionary ladies. "I want," he said, "some sort of religious communion between men of different faiths."

"Quite possible," said Gandhiji, "if there is no mental reservation."

"But a friend of mine, a great humanitarian worker," said Dr. Ceresole, "believes that but for evangelism he should not have taken up his mission work. He gets the driving power from communion with Jesus, he says, because Jesus was always in communion with God."

"The greatest trouble with us is," said Gandhiji, "not that a Christian missionary should rely on his own experience, but that he should dispute the evidence of a Hindu devotee's life. Just as he has his spiritual experience and the joy of communion, even so has a Hindu."

Dr. Ceresole seemed to have no doubt about this, and he said that the broadest view of Christianity seemed to him to have been presented by Frank Lenwood whose book, *Jesus — Lord or Leader*, deserved to be better known than it is. "He says he has the greatest respect for the personality of Jesus, but he thought he might respectfully criticize him."

But the mention of mental reservation led the missionary visitors to raise the question of questions, so far as missionaries in India are concerned. "I have not had the time or desire to evangelize," one of them said. "The Church at home would be happy if through our hospital more people would be led to Christian life."

"But whilst you give the medical help you expect the reward in the shape of your patients becoming Christians."

"Yes, the reward is expected. Otherwise there are many other places in the world which need our service. But instead of going there, we come here."

"There is the kink. At the back of your mind there is not pure service for its sake, but the result of service in the shape of many people coming to the Christian fold."

"In my own work there is no ulterior motive. I care for people, I alleviate pain, because I cannot do otherwise. The source of this is my loyalty to Jesus who ministered to suffering humanity. At the back of my mind there is, I admit, the desire that people may find the same joy in Jesus that I find. Where is the kink?"

"The kink is in the Church thinking that there are people in whom certain things are lacking, and that you must supply them whether they want them or not. If you simply say to your patients, 'You have taken the medicine I gave you. Thank God. He has healed you. Don't come again,' you have done your duty. But if you also say, 'How nice it would be if you had the same faith in Christianity as I have,' you do not make of your medicine a free gift."

"But if I feel that I have something medically and spiritually which I can give, how can I keep it?"

"There is a way out of the difficulty. You must feel that what you possess, your patient also can possess but through a different route. You will say to yourself, 'I have come through this route, you may come through a different route.' Why should you want him to pass through your University and no other?"

"Because I have my partiality for my Alma Mater."

"There is my difficulty. Because you adore your mother, you cannot wish that all the rest were your mother's children."

"That is a physical impossibility."

"Then this one is a spiritual impossibility. God has the whole of humanity as his children. How can I limit God's grace by my little mind and say this is the only way?"

"I do not say it is the only way. There might be a better way."

"If you concede that there might be a better way, you have surrendered your point."

"Well if you say that you have found your way, I am not so terrifically concerned with you. I will deal with one who is floundering in mud."

"Will you judge him? Have you people not floundered? Why will you present your particular brand of truth to all?"

"I must present to them the medicine I know."

"Then you will say to him, 'Have you seen your own doctor?' You will send him to his doctor, and ask the doctor to take charge of him. You will perhaps consult that doctor, you will discuss with him the diagnosis, and will convince him or allow yourself to be convinced by him. But there you are dealing with a wretched physical thing. Here we are dealing with a spiritual thing where you cannot go through all these necessary investigations. What I plead for is humanity. You do not claim freedom from hypocrisy for the Christian Church?"

Dr. Ceresole: "Most of us believe our religion to be the best, and they have not the slightest idea of what other religions have revealed to their adherents. Dr.— has made a careful study of the Hindu scriptures, and he has observed what Hinduism gives to the Hindus."

"I say it is not enough for him to read the Song Celestial or the Koran. It is necessary for him to read the Koran with Islamic spectacles and the Gita with Hindu spectacles, just as he would expect me to read the Bible with Christian spectacles. I would ask him: 'Have you read the Gita as reverently as I have or even as reverently as I have read the Bible?' I tell you I have not read as many books on Hinduism as I have about Christianity. And yet I did not come to the conclusion that Christianity or Hinduism was the *only* way."

Gandhiji discussed the instance of Mr. Stokes—now Shri Satyanand—who was in his early years in India nearly killed for preaching Christianity to the Pathans, but who in a truly Christian spirit secured his assailant's reprieve, and who in the later years said to himself, "My faith in Jesus is as bright as ever, but I cannot deliver the message of Jesus to the Hindus unless I become a Hindu. Unless I make the Hindus better Hindus I shall not," he said, "be true to my Lord."

But, then, wondered the missionary friends, what exactly should be the missionaries' attitude?

"I think," said Gandhiji, "I have made it clear. But I shall say it again in other words: *Just to forget that you have come to a country of heathens, and to think that they are as much in search of God as you are; just to feel that you are not going there to give your spiritual goods to them, but that you will share your worldly goods of which you have a good stock. You will then do your work without a mental reservation and thereby you will share your spiritual treasures. The knowledge that you have this reservation creates a barrier between you and me.*"

"Do you think that, because of what you call that mental reservation, the work that one could accomplish would suffer?"

"I am sure. You would not be half as useful as you would be without the reservation. The reservation means that you belong to a different and a higher species, and you make yourself inaccessible to others."

"A barrier would be certainly my Western way of living."

"No, that can be immediately broken."

"Would you be really happy if we stayed at home?"

"I cannot say that. But I will certainly say that I have never been able to understand your going out of America. Is there nothing to do there?"

"Even in America there is enough scope for educational work."

"That is a fatal confession. You are not a superfluity there. But for the curious position that your Church has taken, you would not be here."

"I have come because the Indian women need medical care to a greater extent than American women do. But coupled with that I have a desire to share my Christian heritage."

"That is exactly the position I have been trying to counter. You have already said that there may be a better way."

"No, I meant to say that there may be a better way fifty years hence."

"Well we were talking of the present, and you said there might be a better way."

"No, there is no better way today than the one I am following."

"That is what I say is assuming too much. You have not examined all religious beliefs. But even if you had, you may not claim infallibility. You assume knowledge of all people, which you can do only if you were God. I want you to understand that you are laboring under a double fallacy: That what you think is best for you is really so; and that what you regard as the best for you is the best for the whole world. It is an assumption of omniscience and infallibility. I plead for a little humility."

Mahadev Desai in *Harijan*, July 18, 1936

TRUE EVANGELISM

Do you see a reason for Christian workers in the West to come here, and, if so, what is their contribution?

Gandhi: In the manner in which they are working, there would seem to be no room for them. Quite unconsciously, they do harm to themselves and so to us. It is, perhaps, impertinent for me to say that they do harm to themselves, but quite pertinent to say that they do harm to us. They do harm to those amongst whom they work and those amongst whom they do not work, i.e., the harm is done to the whole of India. They present a Christianity of their belief, but not the message of Jesus as I understand it. The more I study their activities the more sorry I become. There is such a gross misunderstanding of religion on the part of those who are intelligent, very far advanced, and whose motives need not be questioned. It is a tragedy that such a thing should happen in the human family.

WORK IN A RELIGIOUS SPIRIT

You are referring to things as they are at present. Do you visualize a situation in which there is a different approach?

Gandhi: Your ability is unquestioned. You can utilize all those abilities for the service of India which she would appreciate. That can only happen if there are no mental reservations. If you come to give education, you must give it after the Indian pattern. You should sympathetically study our institutions and suggest changes. But you come with preconceived notions and seek to destroy. If people from the West came on Indian terms, they would supply a felt want. When Americans come and ask me what service they can render, I tell them: "If you dangle your millions before us, you will make beggars of us and demoralize us. But in one thing I do not mind being a beggar. I would beg of you your scientific talent. You can ask your engineers and agricultural experts to place their services at our disposal." They must not come to us as our lords and masters, but as volunteer workers. A paid servant would throw up his job any day, but a volunteer worker could not do so. If such come, the more the merrier. A Mysore engineer (who is a Pole) has sent me a box of handmade tools made to suit village requirements. Supposing an engineer of that character comes and studies our tools and our cottage machines and suggests improvements in them, he would be of great service. If you do this kind of work in a religious spirit, you will have delivered the message of Jesus.

LIFE IS MORE ELOQUENT THAN LIPS

Apart from the contribution through the realm of scientific achievement, evangelism seems to you to be out of the question in establishing relationships between East and West?

Gandhi: I do say that. But I speak with a mental reservation. I cannot only reconcile myself to—I must recognize —a fact in Nature which it is useless to gainsay: I mean proper evangelization. When you feel you have received peace from your particular interpretation of the Bible, you share it with others. But you do not need to give vocal expression to it. Your whole life is more eloquent than your lips. Language is always an obstacle to the full expression of thought. How, for instance, will you tell a man to read the Bible as *you* read it, how by word of mouth will you transfer to him the light as you receive it from day to day and moment to moment? Therefore, all religions say: "Your life is your speech." If you are humble enough, you will say you cannot adequately represent your religion by speech or pen.

LANGUAGE OF THE SOUL

But may not one, in all humility, say: "I know that my life falls far short of the ideal, let me explain the ideal I stand for?"

Gandhi: You bid goodbye to humility the moment you say that life is not adequate and that you must supplement it by speech. The human species need not go to animals and shout to them: "We are humans." The animals know them as humans. The language of the soul never lends itself to expression. It rises superior to the body. Language is a limitation of the truth which can be only represented by life.

Harijan, December 12, 1936

WITH AN INDIAN MISSIONARY

Have I not a moral right to speak?

Gandhi: It is not a moral right, but a legal right. There is no right but is legal. Divorced from legality, a moral right is a misnomer. And, therefore, you either enforce a right or fight for it. Whereas nobody asserts one's duty. He humbly performs it. I shall take an illustration. You are here. You feel like preaching to me the Gospel. I deny the right and ask you to go away. If you regard praying for me a duty, you will quietly go away and pray for me. But if you claim the right to preach to me, you will call the police and appeal to them for preventing my obstructing you. That leads to a clash. But your duty no one dare question. You perform it here or elsewhere, and if your prayers to God to change my heart are genuine, God will change my heart. What Christianity, according to my interpretation of it, expects you to do is to pray to God to change my heart. Duty is a debt. Right belongs to a creditor, and it would be a funny thing indeed if a devout Christian claimed to be a creditor!

SPREAD YOUR PERFUME

We do not preach any theology. We simply talk of the life of Christ and what a comfort His life and teaching have been to us. He has been our guide, we say, and ask others also to accept Him as their guide.

Gandhi: Oh yes, do say that. But when you say I must accept Jesus in preference to Ramakrishna Paramahamsa, you will have to go into deep waters. That is why I say let your life speak to us, even as the rose needs no speech but simply spreads its perfume. Even the blind who do not see the rose perceive its fragrance. That is the secret of the gospel of the rose. But the Gospel that Jesus preached is more subtle and fragrant than the gospel of the rose. If the rose needs no agent, much less does the Gospel of Christ need any agent.

Let us think of the bulk of your people who preach the Gospel. Do they spread the perfume of their lives? That is to me the sole criterion. All I want them to do is to live Christian lives, not to annotate them. I have come to this view after laborious and prayerful search, and I am glad to say that there is a growing body of Christians who accept my view.

Harijan, April 7, 1937

A TALK WITH CHRISTIAN FRIENDS

Some Christian friends visited Sevagram during the first week of this month. One of them, a professor from the South, was developing before Gandhiji the case for conversion from a Christian missionary's standpoint.

"As a Christian," he began, "I believe that God Himself entered the world in the form of Jesus Christ. I place Jesus Christ in the position of God-man. He differs from all other prophets not in degree only but in kind. He is God incarnate and the only incarnation of God. I know Hindus and Muslims, so long as they are Hindus and Muslims, cannot share this position. But as a servant of Jesus Christ and his Gospel I can hold no other. The Christ founded a visible organic society on earth, not merely an invisible bond of union in sacrament. I claim the right to preach the truth of Jesus Christ by word and life. I must pray that the hearts of all people may behold in Jesus God incarnate and be led to enter His visible Church. And so the Christians strive and labor to that end. This right of propagation of the gospel is part of our religious freedom. Will you under Swaraj allow Christians to go on with their proselytizing activity without any hindrance?" He paused for a reply.

"No legal hindrance," replied Gandhiji, "can be put in the way of any Christian or of anybody preaching for the acceptance of his doctrine."

The visitor was anxious to know whether the freedom they were having under the British regime would be allowed them under the national Government without any interference.

"I can't answer that question categorically," replied Gandhiji, "because I do not know what is exactly allowed and what is not allowed under the British regime today. That is a legal question. Besides, what is permitted may not necessarily be the same thing as what is *permissible* under the law. All, therefore, I can say is that you should enjoy all the freedom you are entitled to under the law today."

Gandhiji's visitor said, "Our position is that, holding the viewpoint that we do, we cannot give up our mission work as we are today carrying it out, even under persecution. Some of us are under an apprehension that they may have hereafter to labor under such disabilities. Is there any guarantee that such a thing would not happen?"

"As I wrote in *Harijan*," replied Gandhiji, "you do not seem to realize that Christians are today enjoying privileges because they are Christians. The moment a person here turns Christian, he becomes a *Saheb log*. He almost changes his nationality. He gets a job and position which he could not have otherwise got. He adopts foreign dress and ways of living. He cuts himself off from his own people and begins to fancy himself a limb of the ruling class. What the Christians are afraid of losing, therefore, is not their rights but anomalous privileges."

The visitor admitted the truth of Gandhiji's remarks, but assured him that whatever might have been the case in the past, Christians as a class no longer wished to retain any exceptional privileges.

Another missionary friend recalling Gandhiji's well-known objection to the prevailing proselytizing practices chimed in: "Why may not I share with others my experience of Jesus Christ which has given me such an ineffable peace?"

"Because," replied Gandhiji, "you cannot possibly say that what is best for you is best for all. Quinine may be the only means of saving life in your case, but a dangerous poison in the case of another. And again, is it not superarrogation to assume that you alone possess the key to spiritual joy and peace, and that an adherent of a different faith cannot get the same in equal measure from a study of his scripture? I enjoy a peace and equanimity of spirit which has excited the envy of many Christian friends. I have got it principally through the Gita.

"Your difficulty lies in your considering the other faiths as false or so adulterated as to amount to falsity. And you shut your eyes to the truth that shines in the other faiths and which gives equal joy and peace to their votaries. I have not hesitated, therefore, to recommend to my Christian friends a prayerful and sympathetic study of the other scriptures of the world. I can give my own humble testimony that, whilst such study has enabled me to give the same respect to them that I give to my own, it has enriched my own faith and broadened my vision."

Gandhiji's interlocutor was silent. "What would be your message to a

Christian like me and my fellows?" the professor finally asked. Gandhiji replied, "Become worthy of the message that is imbedded in the Sermon on the Mount, and join the spinning brigade."

Pyarelal in *Harijan*, January 13, 1940

—— Chapter Four ——

All Religions Are True

FOUNDATION OF FELLOWSHIP

In order to attain a perfect fellowship, every act of its members must be a religious act and an act of sacrifice. I came to the conclusion long ago, after prayerful search and study and discussion with as many people as I could meet, that all religions were true, and also, that all had some error in them; and that whilst I hold by my own, I should hold others as dear as Hinduism; from which it logically follows that we should hold all as dear as our nearest kith and kin and that we should make no distinction between them. So, we can only pray, if we are Hindus, not that a Christian should become a Hindu; or if we are Mussalmans, not that a Hindu, or a Christian should become a Mussalman; nor should we even secretly pray that anyone should be converted; but our inmost prayer should be that a Hindu should be a better Hindu, a Muslim a better Muslim, and a Christian a better Christian. That is the fundamental truth of fellowship.

If, however, there is any suspicion in your minds that only one religion can be true and others false, you must reject the doctrine of fellowship. Then, we would have a continuous process of exclusion and found our fellowship on an exclusive basis. Above all, I plead for utter truthfulness. If we do not feel for other religions as we feel for our own, we had better disband ourselves, for we do not want a wishy-washy toleration. My doctrine of toleration does not include toleration of evil, though it does the toleration of the evil-minded. It does not, therefore, mean that you have to invite each and every one who is evil-minded to tolerate a false faith. By a true faith I mean one the sum total of whose energy is for the good of its adherents; by a false I mean that which is predominantly false. If you, therefore, feel that the sum total of Hinduism has been bad for the Hindus and the world, you must reject it as a false faith.

I would not only not try to convert, but would not even secretly pray that anyone should embrace my faith. My prayer would always be that Imamsaheb should be a better Mussalman, or become the best he can.

57

Hinduism, with its message of Ahimsa is to me the most glorious religion in the world — as my wife to me is the most beautiful woman in the world — but others may feel the same about their own religion. Cases of real honest conversion are quite possible. If some people, for their inward satisfaction and growth, change their religion, let them do so.

Young India, May 29, 1924

A SACRED DUTY

Gandhi was criticized by certain correspondents for reading from the New Testament in an address to college students. He responded as follows.

I hold that it is the duty of every cultured man or woman to read sympathetically the scriptures of the world. If we are to respect others' religions as we would have them to respect our own, a friendly study of the world's religions is a sacred duty. We need not dread, upon our grown-up children, the influence of scriptures other than our own. We liberalize their outlook upon life by encouraging them to study freely all that is clean. Fear there would be when someone reads his own scriptures to young people with intention secretly or openly of converting them. He must then be biased in favor of his own scriptures. For myself, I regard my study of and reverence for the Bible, the Koran, and the other scriptures to be wholly consistent with my claim to be a staunch Sanatani Hindu. He is no Sanatani Hindu who is narrow, bigoted, and considers evil to be good if it has the sanction of antiquity and is to be found supported in any Sanskrit book. I claim to be a staunch Sanatani Hindu because, though I reject all that offends my moral sense, I find the Hindu scriptures to satisfy the needs of the soul. My respectful study of other religions has not abated my reverence for or my faith in the Hindu scriptures. They have indeed left their deep mark upon my understanding of the Hindu scriptures. They have broadened my view of life. They have enabled me to understand more clearly many an obscure passage in the Hindu scriptures.

The charge of being a Christian in secret is not new. It is both a libel and a compliment — a libel because there are men who can believe me to be capable of being secretly anything, i.e., for fear of being that openly. There is nothing in the world that would keep me from professing Christianity or any other faith, the moment I felt the truth of and the need for it. Where there is fear there is no religion. The charge is a compliment in that it is a reluctant acknowledgement of my capacity for appreciating the beauties of Christianity. Let me own this. If I could call myself, say, a Christian or a Mussalman, with my own interpretation of the Bible or the Koran, I should not hesitate to call myself either. For then Hindu, Christian, and Mussalman would be synonymous terms. I do believe that in the other world there are neither Hindus nor Christians nor Mussalmans. There all are judged not according to their labels or professions but according to their actions irrespective of their professions. During our earthly existence there will always be these labels. I therefore prefer to retain the label of my forefathers so long as it does not cramp my growth and does not debar me from assimilating all that is good anywhere else.

Young India, September 2, 1926

PLEA FOR TOLERATION

In spite of my being a staunch Hindu, I find room in my faith for Christian and Islamic and Zoroastrian teaching, and, therefore, my Hinduism seems to some to be a conglomeration and some have even dubbed me as eclectic. Well, to call a man eclectic is to say that he has no faith, but mine is a broad faith which does not oppose Christians—not even a Plymouth Brother—not even the most fanatical Mussalman. It is a faith based on the broadest possible toleration. I refuse to abuse a man for his fanatical deeds, because I try to see them from his point of view. It is that broad faith that sustains me. It is a somewhat embarrassing position, I know—but to others, not to me.

I should love all the men—not only in India but in the world—belonging to the different faiths, to become better people by contact with one another, and if that happens the world will be a much better place to live in than it is today. I plead for the broadest toleration, and I am working to that end. I ask people to examine every religion from the point of the religionists themselves. I do not expect the India of my dream to develop one religion, i.e., to be wholly Hindu or wholly Christian, or wholly Mussalman; but I want it to be wholly tolerant, with its religions working side by side with one another.

Young India, December 22, 1927

THINGS OF THE SPIRIT

I am very much attracted by your illustration of the smell of a rose. We will all admit that the real proof of the truth of a religion is the fragrance of real spirituality, love, joy, peace, that may emanate from those that hold to that religion. And without that our creeds and professions and preaching of it, even our worship and prayers, will not lead anyone to see that we have "a secret of the Lord" with us. But does it follow from this that we cannot impart a share of what we rejoice in to others in any other way than as the smell of a rose imparts itself?

Gandhi: Let me extend the analogy of fragrance, faulty as all analogies are in their very nature. The rose imparts its fragrance not in many ways but only one. Those who have not the sense of smell will miss it. You cannot feel the fragrance through the tongue or the ear or the skin. So may you not receive spirituality except through the spiritual sense. Hence have all religions recognized the necessity of that sense being awakened. It is a second birth. A man with intense spirituality may, without speech or a gesture, touch the hearts of millions who have never seen him and whom he has never seen. The most eloquent preacher, if he has not spirituality in him, will fail to touch the hearts of his audience. Therefore, I venture to think that most of the effort of modern missions is not only useless but more often than not harmful.

At the root of missionary effort is also the assumption that one's own belief is true, not only for oneself but for all the world; whereas the truth is that God reaches us through millions of ways not understood by us. In missionary effort, therefore, there is lack of real humility that instinctively recognizes human limitations and the limitless powers of God. I have no feeling that, from a spiritual standpoint, I am necessarily superior to the so-called savage. And spiritual superiority is a dangerous thing to feel. It is not like many other things which we can perceive, analyze, and prove through our senses. If it is there, I cannot be deprived of it by any power on earth, and it will have its effect in its own due time. But if, in matters of medicine and other natural sciences, I feel my superiority over others, a thing of which I may be legitimately conscious, and if I have love for my fellow-beings, I would naturally share my knowledge with them. But things of the spirit I leave to God and thus keep the bond between fellow-beings and myself pure, correct within limits. But I must not carry this argument any further.

Young India, March 22, 1928

LETTERS TO A CHRISTIAN

The following selections are from letters to Esther Fearing, a Danish missionary who was attracted to Sabarmati, one of Gandhi's ashrams.

CHRISTIAN CHARITY

You have to summon to your aid all your Christian charity to be able to return largeness against pettiness. And we are truly large only when we are that joyfully. I have known friends being generous in a miserable spirit. Their generosity has become a kind of martyrdom. To rejoice in suffering, to pity the person who slights you, and to love him all the more for his weakness, is really charity. But we may not be able to reach that stage. Then, we should not experiment. And so, my dear Esther, if you find "A" trying your nerves, you must avoid the close association. On no account shall I have you to lose your inward peace and joy. I want you so to order your life that the Ashram gives you greater joy, greater happiness and finer perception of Truth. I want you to be a greater Christian for being in the Ashram. You were with me the whole of yesterday and during the night. I shall pray that you may be healthier in mind, body and spirit so as to be a better instrument of His service.

THE PRESENCE OF GOD

As I have already said, you have come to the Ashram not to lose your Christianity, but to perfect it. If you do not feel the presence of God at the prayer meetings, then remember that the names Rama and Krishna signify the same as Jesus to you.

Your coming is a joy to me. It will be a greater joy if, upon experience, you find it gives you peace, health and real joy and if it thereby enables the other Christians to see that God and Christianity can be found also in institutions that do not call themselves Christian, and that Truth is the same in all religions though, through refraction, it appears for the time being variegated even as light does through a prism.

MEANING OF "RESIST NOT EVIL"

"Resist not evil" has a much deeper meaning than appears on the surface. The evil in "A," for instance, must not be resisted; you or, for that matter, I must not fret over it or be impatient and say to ourselves: "Why will not this woman see the truth or return the love I give her?" She can no more go against her nature than a leopard can change his spots. If you or I love, we act according to our nature. If she does not respond she acts according to hers. And if we worry, we "resist evil." I feel *that* is the deeper meaning of the injunction. And so, in your dealings with everybody I want you to keep your equanimity.

THE UNIQUENESS OF JESUS

In spite of most devout attention to every word ascribed to Jesus in the New Testament, and in spite of my having read in a humble spirit all about Jesus, I have really not seen any fundamental distinction between Jesus and the other teachers I can understand, explain, and appreciate. Nobody taught me in my childhood to differentiate. I have, therefore, grown without bias one way or the other. I can pay equal homage to Jesus, Mohammed, Krishna, Buddha, Zoroaster, and others that may be named. But this is not a matter for argument. It is a matter for each one's deep and sacred conviction. I have no desire whatsoever to dislodge you from the exclusive homage you pay to Jesus. But I would like you to understand and appreciate the other inclusive position.

THE CROSS MAKES A UNIVERSAL APPEAL

The Cross, undoubtedly, makes a universal appeal the moment you give it a universal meaning in place of the narrow one that is often heard at ordinary meetings. But, then, you have to have the eyes of the soul with which to contemplate it.

My Dear Child, pp. 39, 45, 50, 86, 100

EQUALITY OF RELIGIONS

The following reflections were written during a period of detention in Yeravda prison. They were published in a volume entitled *From Yeravda Mandir* ("From Yeravda Temple").

Ahimsa teaches us to entertain the same respect for the religious faiths of others as we accord to our own, thus admitting the imperfection of the latter. This admission will be readily made by a seeker of Truth, who follows the Law of Love. If we had attained the full vision of Truth, we would no longer be mere seekers, but would have become one with God, for Truth is God. But being only seekers, we prosecute our quest, and are conscious of our imperfection. And if we are imperfect ourselves, religion as conceived by us must also be imperfect.

ALL FAITHS ARE IMPERFECT

We have not realized religion in its perfection, even as we have not realized God. Religion of our conception, being thus imperfect, is always subject to a process of evolution and reinterpretation. Progress towards Truth, towards God, is possible only because of such evolution. And if all faiths outlined by men are imperfect, the question of comparative merit does not arise. All faiths constitute a revelation of Truth, but all are imperfect, and liable to error. Reverence for other faiths need not blind us to their faults. We must be keenly alive to the defects of our own faiths also, yet not leave it on that account, but try to overcome those defects. Looking at all religions with an equal eye, we would not only hesitate, but would think it our duty to blend into our faith every acceptable feature of other faiths.

WHY ARE THERE DIFFERENT FAITHS?

The question then arises: Why should there be so many different faiths? The Soul is one, but the bodies which She animates are many. We cannot reduce the number of bodies; yet we recognize the unity of the Soul. Even as a tree has a single trunk, but many branches and leaves, so is there one true and perfect Religion, but it becomes many, as it passes through the human medium. The one Religion is beyond all speech. Imperfect men put it into such languages as they can command, and their words are interpreted by other men equally imperfect. Whose interpretation is to be held to be the right one? Everybody is right from his own standpoint, but it is not impossible that everybody is wrong. Hence the necessity for tolerance, which does not mean indifference towards one's own faith, but a more intelligent and purer love for it. Tolerance gives us spiritual insight, which is as far from fanaticism as the North Pole from the South. True knowledge of religion breaks down the barriers between faith and faith. Cultivation of tolerance for other faiths will impart to us a truer understanding of our own.

Tolerance obviously does not disturb the distinction between right and wrong, or good and evil. The reference here throughout is naturally to the principal faiths of the world. They are all based on common fundamentals. They have all produced great saints.

EQUIMINDEDNESS

When I was turning over the pages of the sacred books of different faiths for my own satisfaction, I became sufficiently familiar for my purpose with Christianity, Islam, Zoroastrianism, Judaism, and Hinduism. In reading these texts, I can say, I was equiminded towards all these faiths, although perhaps I was not then conscious of it. Refreshing my memory of those days, I do not find I ever had the slightest desire to criticize any of those religions merely because they were not my own, but read each sacred book in a spirit of reverence, and found the same fundamental morality in each. Some things I did not understand then, and do not understand even now, but experience has taught me that it is a mistake hastily to imagine that anything that we cannot understand is necessarily wrong. Some things which I did not understand first have since become as clear as daylight. Equimindedness helps us to solve many difficulties and even when we criticize anything, we express ourselves with a humility and a courtesy which leave no sting behind them.

THE GOLDEN RULE

The acceptance of the doctrine of Equality of Religions does not abolish the distinction between religion and irreligion. We do not propose to cultivate toleration for irreligion. That being so, some people might object that there would be no room left for equimindedness, if everyone took his own decision as to what was religion and what was irreligion. If we follow the Law of Love, we shall not bear any hatred towards the irreligious brother. On the contrary, we shall love him, and therefore, either we shall bring him to see the error of his ways, or he will point out our error, or each will tolerate the other's difference of opinion. If the other party does not observe the Law of Love, he may be violent to us. If, however, we cherish real love for him, it will overcome his bitterness in the end. All obstacles in our path will vanish, if only we observe the golden rule that we must not be impatient with those whom we may consider to be in error, but must be prepared, if need be, to suffer in our own person.

From Yeravda Mandir, 1930, Chaps. X, XI

A STRANGE SEEKER

Professor Krzenski from Poland was a rather strange specimen of a seeker of truth that I came across the other day. He said to Gandhiji that he had found much spirituality in India, and was wondering if all the spiritual forces of the world could not combine to conquer the materialistic forces that were gathering strong in India. But Catholicism, according to him, is the only true religion, and the only spiritual force. As a professor of philosophy he had studied all the religious systems of the world and had come to this deliberate conclusion!

"Do you therefore say that other religions are untrue?" Gandhiji asked him.

"If others are convinced that their religions are true, they are saved," said the professor, meaning to say that that conviction was impossible!

"Therefore," said Gandhiji, "you will say that everyone would be saved even through untruth. For you say that, if a man really and sincerely believes in what is as a matter of fact untruth, he is saved. Would you not also hold, therefore, that your own way may be untrue but that you are convinced that it is true and therefore you will be saved?"

"But I have studied all religions and have found that mine is the only true religion."

"But so have others studied other religions. What about them? Well, I go further and tell you that religion is one and it has several branches which are all equal."

"I accept," said the professor, "that no religion lacks divine inspiration but all have not the same truth, because all have not the same light."

"It is an essentially untrue position to take, for a seeker after truth, that he alone is in absolute possession of truth. What is happening to the poor astronomers today? They are changing their position every day, and there are scientists who impeach even Einstein's latest theory."

"No. But I have examined the arguments in favor of other religions."

"But it is an intellectual examination," said Gandhiji. "You require different scales to weigh spiritual truths. Either we are all untrue—quite a logical position to take—but since truth does not come out of untruth it is better to say that we all have truth but not the complete truth. For God reveals His truth to instruments that are imperfect. Raindrops of purest distilled water become diluted or polluted as soon as they come in contact with Mother Earth. My submission is that your position is arrogant. But I suggest to you a better position. Accept all religions as equal, for all have the same root and the same laws of growth."

But the good professor would still have his way and said, "It is necessary to examine every religion philosophically and find out which is more harmonious, more perfect."

"That presupposes that all religions are in watertight compartments.

That is wrong. They are always growing," rejoined Gandhiji. "Let us not limit God's function. He may reveal Himself in a thousand ways and a thousand times."

Now the professor switched on to the next question, viz. that of fighting materialism.

"Well," said Gandhiji, "it is no use trying to fight these forces without giving up the idea of conversion, which I assure you is the deadliest poison that ever sapped the fountain of truth."

"But," said the professor, "I have a great respect for your religion."

"Not enough," said Gandhiji. "I had that feeling myself one day, but I found that it was not enough. Unless I accept the position that all religions are equal, and I have as much regard for other religions as I have for my own, I would not be able to live in the boiling war around me. Any make-believe combination of spiritual forces is doomed to failure if this fundamental position is not accepted. I read and get all my inspiration from the Gita. But I also read the Bible and the Koran to enrich my own religion. I incorporate all that is good in other religions."

"That is your goodwill."

"That is not enough."

"But I have great respect for you."

"Not enough. If I were to join the Catholic Church, you would have greater respect for me."

"Oh yes," said the professor with engaging naivete, "if you became a Catholic, you would be as great as St. Francis."

"But not otherwise? A Hindu cannot be a St. Francis? Poor Hindu!"

And there was loud laughter in which the professor joined.

Mahadev Desai in *Harijan*, January 16, 1937

BRANCHES OF THE SAME TREE

For me, the different religions are beautiful flowers from the same garden, or they are branches of the same majestic tree. Therefore, they are equally true, though being received and interpreted through human instruments equally imperfect. It is impossible for me to reconcile myself to the idea of conversion after the style that goes on in India and elsewhere today. It is an error which is, perhaps, the greatest impediment to the world's progress towards peace. "Warring creeds" is a blasphemous expression. And it fitly describes the state of things in India, the Mother—as I believe her to be—of Religion or religions. If she is truly the Mother, the motherhood is on trial. Why should a Christian want to convert a Hindu to Christianity and vice versa? Why should he not be satisfied if the Hindu is a good or godly man? If the morals of a man are a matter of no concern, the form of worship in a particular manner in a church, a mosque, or a temple is an empty formula; it may even be a hindrance to individual or social growth, and insistence on a particular form or repetition of a credo may be a potent cause of violent quarrels leading to bloodshed and ending in utter disbelief in Religion, i.e., God Himself.

Harijan, January 30, 1937

WITH AN AMERICAN CLERGYMAN

Gandhi was visited by a Dr. Crane, a Protestant minister and committed pacifist, who sought Gandhi's attitude toward Christianity and religion in general.

Gandhi answered: "For a time I struggled with the question, 'Which was the true religion out of those I knew?' but ultimately I came to the deliberate conviction that there was no such thing as only one true religion and every other false. There is no religion that is absolutely perfect. All are equally imperfect or more or less perfect. Hence the conclusion that Christianity is as good and true as my own religion. But so also is Islam or Zoroastrianism or Judaism.

"I therefore do not take as literally true the text that Jesus is the only begotten son of God. God cannot be the exclusive Father and I cannot ascribe exclusive divinity to Jesus. He is as divine as Krishna or Rama or Mohammed or Zoroaster. Similarly I do not regard every word of the Bible as the inspired word of God, even as I do not regard every word of the Vedas or the Koran as inspired. The sum total of each of these books is certainly inspired, but I miss that inspiration in many of the things taken individually. The Bible is as much a book of religion with me as the Gita and the Koran.

"Therefore," said Gandhi, "I am not interested in weaning you from Christianity and making you a Hindu, and I would not relish your designs upon me, if you had any, to convert me to Christianity! I would also dispute your claim that Christianity is the only true religion. It is also a true religion, a noble religion, and along with other religions it has contributed to raise the moral height of mankind. But it has yet to make a greater contribution. After all, what are 2,000 years in the life of a religion? Just now Christianity comes to yearning mankind in a tainted form. Fancy bishops supporting slaughter in the name of Christianity!"

"But," asked Dr. Crane, "when you say that all religions are true, what do you do when there are conflicting counsels?"

"I have no difficulty," said Gandhiji, "in hitting upon the truth, because I go by certain fundamental maxims. Truth is superior to everything, and I reject what conflicts with it. Similarly that which is in conflict with non-violence should be rejected. And on matters which can be reasoned out that which conflicts with Reason must also be rejected."

"In matters which can be reasoned out?"

"Yes, there are subjects where Reason cannot take us far and we have to accept things on faith. Faith then does not contradict Reason but transcends it. Faith is a kind of sixth sense which works in cases which are

without the purview of Reason. Well then, given these three criteria, I can
have no difficulty in examining all claims made on behalf of religion. Thus
to believe that Jesus is the only begotten son of God is to me against
Reason, for God can't marry and beget children. The word 'son' there can
only be used in a figurative sense. In that sense everyone who stands in the
position of Jesus is a begotten son of God. If a man is spiritually miles
ahead of us, we may say that he is in a special sense the son of God, though
we are all children of God. We repudiate the relationship in our lives,
whereas his life is a witness to that relationship."

"Then you will recognize degrees of divinity. Would you not say that
Jesus was the most divine?"

"No, for the simple reason that we have no data. Historically we have
more data about Mohammed than anyone else because he was more recent
in time. For Jesus there is less data and still less for Buddha, Rama, and
Krishna; and when we know so little about them, is it not preposterous to
say that one of them was more divine than another? In fact even if there
were a great deal of data available, no judge should shoulder the burden
of sifting all the evidence, if only for this reason that it requires a highly
spiritual person to gauge the degree of divinity of the subjects he examines.
To say that Jesus was 99 per cent divine, and Muhammad 50 per cent, and
Krishna 10 per cent, is to arrogate to oneself a function which really does
not belong to man."

"But," said Dr. Crane, "let us take a debatable point. Supposing I was
debating between whether violence is justified or not. Mohammadanism
would say one thing, Christianity another."

"Then I must decide with the help of the tests I have suggested."

"But does not Muhammad prescribe the use of the sword in certain
circumstances?"

"I suppose most Muslims will agree. But I read religion in a different
way. Khansaheb Abdul Gaffar Khan* derives his belief in nonviolence from
the Koran, and the Bishop of London derives his belief in violence from
the Bible. I derive my belief in nonviolence from the Gita, whereas there
are others who read violence in it. But if the worst came to the worst and
if I came to the conclusion that the Koran teaches violence, I would still
reject violence, but I would not therefore say that the Bible is superior to
the Koran or that Muhammad is inferior to Jesus. It is not my function to
judge Mohammed and Jesus. It is enough that my nonviolence is independent of the sanction of scriptures. But the fact remains that religious
books have a hold upon mankind which other books have not. They have
made a greater impression on me than Mark Twain or, to take a more
appropriate instance, Emerson. Emerson was a thinker. Jesus and Muhammad were through and through men of action in a sense Emerson would

---

* Abdul Gaffar Khan was a Muslim Pathan chief in northwest India and one of the most
resolute followers of Gandhian nonviolence. He was known as the "Frontier Gandhi."

never be. Their power was derived from their faith in God."

"I will take a concrete instance now to show what I mean," said Dr. Crane. "I was terribly shocked on Monday. I counted 37 cows slain on the streets by Muslims in the name of religion, and in offense to the Hindu sentiment. I asked the Hindu friend who travelled with me why the Muslims did so. He said it was part of their religion. 'Is it part of their spiritual growth?' I asked him. He said it was. I met a Mussalman who said, 'We please both God and ourselves.' Now here was a Mussalman revelling in a thing that outrages you and me too. Do you think all this is counter to the Koran?"

"I do indeed," said Gandhiji, and he referred Dr. Crane to the article he had written only last week. "Just as many Hindu practices — e.g. untouchability — are no part of Hindu religion, I say that cow slaughtering is no part of Islam. But I do not wrestle with the Muslims who believe that it is part of Islam."

"What do you say to the attempts to convert?"

"I strongly resent these overtures to utterly ignorant men. I can perhaps understand overtures made to me, as indeed they are being made. For they can reason with me and I can reason with them. But I certainly resent the overtures made to Harijans. When a Christian preacher goes and says to a Harijan that Jesus was the only begotten Son of God, he will give him a blank stare. Then he holds all kinds of inducements which debase Christianity."

"Would you say a Harijan is not capable of reason?"

"He is. For instance, if you try to take work out of him without payment, he will not give it. He also has a sense of ethical values. But when you ask him to understand theological beliefs and categories he will not understand anything. I could not do so even when I was seventeen and had a fair share of education and training. The orthodox Hindus have so horribly neglected the Harijan that it is astonishing how he adheres to the Hindu faith. Now I say it is outrageous for others to shake his faith."

"What about a man who says he is commanded by God to do violence?"

"There you would not put another God before him. You need not disturb his religion, but you will disturb his reason."

"But take Hitler. He says he is carrying out God's behest in persecuting the Jews and killing his opponents."

"You will not pit one word of God against another word of God. But you will have to bear down his reason. For him you will have to produce a miracle which you will do when Christians will learn the art of dying without killing in defense of what they hold dearer than religion. But we can go on arguing like this endlessly. And then I may tell you that you are talking against time." And with this Gandhiji looked at his watch.

"Just one question, then. Would you say then that your religion is a synthesis of all religions?"

"Yes, if you will. But I would call that synthesis Hinduism, and for you the synthesis will be Christianity. If I did not do so, you would always be patronizing me, as many Christians do now, saying, 'How nice it would be if Gandhi accepted Christianity,' and Muslims would be doing the same saying, 'How nice it would be if Gandhi accepted Islam!' That immediately puts a barrier between you and me. Do you see that?"

Mahadev Desai in Harijan, March 6, 1937

ONE'S OWN RELIGION

The closest, though very incomplete, analogy for religion I can find is marriage. It is or used to be an indissoluble tie. Much more so is the tie of religion. And just as a husband does not remain faithful to his wife, or wife to her husband, because either is conscious of some exclusive superiority of the other over the rest of his or her sex but because of some indefinable but irresistible attraction, so does one remain irresistibly faithful to one's own religion and find full satisfaction in such adhesion. And just as a faithful husband does not need in order to sustain his faithfulness, to consider other women as inferior to his wife, so does not a person belonging to one religion need to consider others to be inferior to his own.

To pursue the analogy still further, even as faithfulness to one's wife does not presuppose blindness to her shortcomings, so does not faithfulness to one's religion presuppose blindness to the shortcomings of that religion. Indeed, faithfulness, not blind adherence, demands a keener perception of shortcomings and therefore a livelier sense of the proper remedy for their removal. Taking the view I do of religion, it is unnecessary for me to examine the beauties of Hinduism. The reader may rest assured that I am not likely to remain Hindu if I was not conscious of its many beauties. Only for my purpose they need not be exclusive. My approach to other religions, therefore, is never as a fault-finding critic but as a devotee hoping to find the like beauties in other religions and wishing to incorporate in my own the good I may find in them and miss in mine.

Harijan, August 12, 1933

After long study and experience, I have come to the conclusion that (1) all religions are true; (2) all religions have some error in them; (3) all religions are almost as dear to me as my own Hinduism, inasmuch as all human beings should be as dear to me as one's own close relatives. My own veneration for other faiths is the same as that for my own faith.

Sabarmati, 1928, p. 17

I do dimly perceive that whilst everything around me is ever changing, ever dying, there is underlying all that change a living power that is changeless, that holds all together, that creates, dissolves, and recreates. That informing power or spirit is God. And since nothing else I see merely through the senses can or will persist, He alone is.

And is this power benevolent or malevolent? I see it as purely benevolent. For I can see that in the midst of death life persists, in the midst of untruth truth persists, in the midst of darkness light persists. Hence I gather that God is Life, Truth, Light. He is Love. He is the Supreme Good.

But He is no God who merely satisfies the intellect, if He ever does. God to be God must rule the heart and transform it. He must express Himself in even the smallest act of His votary. This can only be done through a definite realization more real than the five senses can ever produce. Sense perceptions can be, often are, false and deceptive, however real they may appear to us. Where there is realization outside the senses it is infallible. It is proved not by extraneous evidence but in the transformed conduct and character of those who have felt the real presence of God within.

Such testimony is to be found in the experience of an unbroken line of prophets and sages in all countries and climes. To reject this evidence is to deny oneself.

This realization is preceded by an immovable faith. He who would in his own person test the fact of God's presence can do so by a living faith. And since faith itself cannot be proved by extraneous evidence, the safest course is to believe in the moral government of the world and therefore in the supremacy of the moral law, the law of Truth and Love. Exercise of faith will be the safest where there is a clear determination summarily to reject all that is contrary to Truth and Love.

I cannot account for the existence of evil by any rational method. To want to do so is to be coequal with God. I am therefore humble enough to recognize evil as such. And I call God long-suffering and patient precisely because He permits evil in the world. I know that He has no evil. He is the author of it and yet untouched by it.

I know too that I shall never know God if I do not wrestle with and against evil even at the cost of life itself. I am fortified in the belief by my own humble and limited experience. The purer I try to become the nearer I feel to be to God. How much more should I be, when my faith is not a mere apology as it is today but has become as immovable as the Himalayas and as white and bright as the snows on their peaks? Meanwhile I invite the correspondent to pray with [John Henry] Newman who sang from experience:

> Lead, kindly light, amid the encircling gloom,
>   Lead Thou me on;
> The night is dark and I am far from home,
>   Lead Thou me on;
> Keep Thou my feet, I do not ask to see
> The distant scene; one step enough for me.

Young India, October 11, 1928

THE NATURE OF GOD

To me God is Truth and Love; God is ethics and morality; God is fear-lessness. God is the source of Light and Life and yet He is above and beyond all these. God is conscience. He is even the atheism of the atheist. For in His boundless love God permits the atheist to live. He is the searcher of hearts. He transcends speech and reason. He knows us and our hearts better than we do ourselves. He does not take us at our word for He knows that we often do not mean it, some knowingly and others unknowingly. He is a personal God to those who need His personal presence. He is embodied to those who need His touch. He is the purest essence. He simply *is* to those who have faith. He is all things to all men.

Young India, March 5, 1925

You have asked me why I consider that God is Truth. In my early youth I was taught to repeat what in Hindu scriptures are known as one thousand names of God. But these one thousand names of God were by no means exhaustive. We believe—and I think it is the truth—that God has as many names as there are creatures and, therefore, we also say that God is name-less and since God has many forms we also consider Him formless, and since He speaks to us through many tongues we consider Him to be speech-less and so on. And so when I came to study Islam I found that Islam too had many names for God. I would say with those who say God is Love, God is Love. But deep down in me I used to say that though God may be Love, God is Truth, above all.

If it is possible for the human tongue to give the fullest description of God, I have come to the conclusion that for myself, God is Truth. But two years ago I went a step further and said that Truth is God. You will see the fine distinction between the two statements, viz. that God is Truth and Truth is God. And I came to that conclusion after a continuous and relent-less search after Truth which began nearly fifty years ago. I then found that the nearest approach to Truth was through Love. But I also found that love has many meanings in the English language at least and that human love in the sense of passion could become a degrading thing also. I found too that love in the sense of Ahimsa had only a limited number of votaries in the world. But I never found a double meaning in connection with truth and even atheists had not demurred to the necessity or power of truth. But in their passion for discovering truth the atheists have not hesitated to deny the very existence of God—from their own point of view rightly. And it was because of this reasoning that I saw that rather than say that God is Truth I should say that Truth is God.

I recall the name of Charles Bradlaugh* who delighted to call himself

* Charles Bradlaugh was a British freethinker and staunch friend of India. Gandhi, along with most Indians living in London, attended his funeral in 1891.

an atheist, but knowing as I do something of him, I would never regard him as an atheist. I would call him a God-fearing man, though I know that he would reject the claim. His face would redden if I would say "Mr. Bradlaugh, you are a truth-fearing man, and so a God-fearing man." I would automatically disarm his criticism by saying that Truth is God, as I have disarmed criticism of many a young man. Add to this the great difficulty that millions have taken the name of God and in His name committed nameless atrocities. Not that scientists very often do not commit cruelties in the name of Truth. I know how in the name of truth and science inhuman cruelties are perpetrated on animals when men perform vivisection. There are thus a number of difficulties in the way, no matter how you describe God. *But the human mind is a limited thing, and you have to labor under limitations when you think of a being or entity who is beyond the power of man to grasp.*

And then we have another thing in Hindu philosophy, viz. God alone is and nothing else exists, and the same truth you find emphasized and exemplified in the Kalma of Islam. There you find it clearly stated that God alone is and nothing else exists. In fact the Sanskrit word for Truth is a word which literally means "that which exists" — *Sat*. For these and several other reasons that I can give you I have come to the conclusion that the definition, "Truth is God," gives me the greatest satisfaction. And when you want to find Truth as God the only inevitable means is Love, i.e. nonviolence, and since I believe that ultimately the means and the end are convertible terms, I should not hesitate to say that God is Love.

"What then is Truth?"

A difficult question, but I have solved it for myself by saying that it is what the voice within tells you. How, then, you ask, do different people think of different and contrary truths? Well, seeing that the human mind works through innumerable media and that the evolution of the human mind is not the same for all, it follows that what may be truth for one may not be truth for another, and hence those who have made these experiments have come to the conclusion that there are certain conditions to be observed in making those experiments. Just as for conducting scientific experiments there is an indispensable scientific course of instruction, in the same way strict preliminary discipline is necessary to qualify a person to make experiments in the spiritual realm. Everyone should, therefore, realize his limitations before he speaks of his Inner Voice. Therefore we have the belief based upon experience, that those who would make individual search after truth as God, must go through several vows, as for instance, the vow of truth, the vow of *Brahmacharya* (purity)—for you cannot possibly divide your love for Truth and God with anything else—the vow of nonviolence, of poverty and nonpossession. Unless you impose on yourselves the five vows you many not embark on the experiment at all. There are several other conditions prescribed, but I must not take you through all of them.

Suffice it to say that those who have made these experiments know that it is not proper for everyone to claim to hear the voice of conscience, and it is because we have at the present moment everybody claiming the right of conscience without going through any discipline whatsoever and there is so much untruth being delivered to a bewildered world, all that I can, in true humility, present to you is that truth is not to be found by anybody who has not got an abundant sense of humility. If you would swim on the bosom of the ocean of Truth you must reduce yourself to a zero. Further than this I cannot go along this fascinating path.

Young India, December 31, 1931

MY RELIGION

I am not a visionary. I claim to be a practical idealist. The religion of nonviolence is not meant merely for the *rishis* and saints. It is meant for the common people as well. Nonviolence is the law of our species as violence is the law of the brute. The spirit lies dormant in the brute, and he knows no law but that of physical might. The dignity of man requires obedience to a higher law—to the strength of the spirit.

I have therefore ventured to place before India the ancient law of self-sacrifice. For Satyagraha and its offshoots, noncooperation and civil resistance, are nothing but new names for the law of suffering. The *rishis* who discovered the law of nonviolence in the midst of violence, were greater geniuses than Newton. They were themselves greater warriors than Wellington. Having themselves known the use of arms, they realized their uselessness, and taught a weary world that its salvation lay not through violence but nonviolence.

Nonviolence in its dynamic condition means conscious suffering. It does not mean meek submission to the will of the evil-doer, but it means putting one's whole soul against the will of the tyrant. Working under this law of our being, it is possible for a single individual to defy the whole might of an unjust empire, to save his honor, his religion, and his soul.

Young India, August 11, 1920

Nonviolence is a perfect state. It is a goal towards which all mankind moves naturally though unconsciously. Man does not become divine when he personifies innocence in himself. Only then does he become truly man. In our present state we are partly men and partly beasts, and in our ignorance and even arrogance say that we truly fulfill the purpose of our species when we deliver blow for blow and develop the measure of anger required for the purpose. We pretend to believe that retaliation is the law of our being, whereas in every scripture we find that retaliation is nowhere obligatory but only permissible. It is restraint that is obligatory. Restraint is the law of our being. For, highest perfection is unattainable without highest restraint. Suffering is thus the badge of the human tribe.

The goal ever recedes from us. The greater the progress, the greater the recognition of our unworthiness. Satisfaction lies in the effort, not in the attainment. Full effort is full victory.

Young India, March 9, 1922

I will give you a talisman. Whenever you are in doubt, or when the self becomes too much with you, try the following expedient:

Recall the face of the poorest and the most helpless man whom you may have seen and ask yourself if the step you contemplate is going to be of any use to him. Will he be able to gain anything by it? Will it restore him to a control over his own life and destiny? In other words, will it lead to Swaraj or self-rule for the hungry and also spiritually starved millions of our countrymen?

Then you will find your doubts and your self melting away.

This Was Bapu, R.K. Prabhu, 1954, p. 48

I have found that life persists in the midst of destruction and therefore there must be a higher law than that of destruction. Only under that law would a well-ordered society be intelligible and life worth living. And if that is the law of life, we have to work it out in daily life. Whenever there are jars, whenever you are confronted with an opponent, conquer him with love — in this crude manner I have worked it out in my life. That does not mean that all my difficulties are solved. Only I have found that this law of love has answered as the law of destruction has never done. The more I work at this law, the more I feel delight in life, delight in the scheme of this universe. It gives me a peace and a meaning of the mysteries of nature that I have no power to describe.

Young India, October 1, 1931

The only way to find God is to see Him in His creation and be one with it. This can only be done by service of all. I am a part and parcel of the whole, and I cannot find Him apart from the rest of humanity. My countrymen are my nearest neighbors. They have become so helpless, so resourceless, so inert that I must concentrate myself on serving them. If I could persuade myself that I should find Him in a Himalayan cave I would proceed there immediately. But I know that I cannot find Him apart from humanity.

Harijan, August 29, 1936

I believe in the message of truth delivered by all the religious teachers of the world. And it is my constant prayer that I may never have a feeling of anger against my traducers, that even if I fall a victim to an assassin's bullet, I may deliver up my soul with the remembrance of me to be written down an imposter if my lips utter a word of anger or abuse against my assailant at the last moment.

Pyaralel, *The Last Phase*, 1958, II:101

— PART TWO —

CHRISTIAN RESPONSE

—— **Chapter Five** ——

Gandhian Guidelines for a World of Religious Difference

Diana L. Eck

Diana Eck is Professor of Comparative Religion and Indian Studies at Harvard University, where she has taught courses on Gandhian philosophy. Her publications include *Benaras, City of Light* and, as co-editor, *Speaking of Faith: Global Perspectives on Women, Religion, and Social Change*. Active for many years in the World Council of Churches, she is currently moderator and chair of the Working Group on Dialogue with People of Living Faiths.

At six-thirty in the morning at Lakshmi Ashram, a Gandhian ashram in the Kumaon district of the Himalayas, two dozen little girls and as many older women in their twenties and thirties begin their day of work with a period of prayer together. It inevitably includes the chanted recitation of the eleven virtues that were part of the daily Gandhian prayer: *"Ahimsa, satya, asteya . . ."* "Nonviolence, truth, non-stealing . . ." Gandhi would have explained that nonviolence is not simply refraining from harm, but being positively motivated by love; that truth is not a possession of any particular group of people, but a gift and a goal; and that non-stealing is not merely refraining from taking things from others, but refraining from owning and using more than one needs. The naming of these common virtues is like a seed-mantra of Gandhian thought, each word unfolding with the distinctive meaning imparted to it by the life of Mahatma Gandhi.

Further down the list in the recitation is *"sarvadharma samanatva,"* "having an equal mind toward all religions," or respect for the religious traditions of others. The phrase lingers in the cool mountain air as the girls go out to work in the vegetable gardens. They could not sing that verse loudly enough in modern India, torn as it is with religiously fired communalism. Sikhs and Hindus escalate the level of violence and threat in the

77

Punjab. Hindus and Muslims spar over the sixteenth-century mosque built on the alleged site of Rama's birthplace in Ayodhya.

The communalist, according to Gandhi, is the one whose spirit of sacrifice is limited to his or her own community and does not extend beyond that immediate community to the common good. In the politicized world of India, it has become commonplace to compete for gains and benefits for one's own religious community by using religious symbols as a rallying cry. However, the Sikh, Hindu, and Muslim communalism that has shaken governments apart in the 1980s is not a new phenomenon in India. Gandhi struggled with it throughout the course of the Indian freedom movement, right through the twenties, thirties, and forties of this century. Indeed, for nearly a thousand years there have been outbursts of religiously related violence and chauvinism, even in this land which has been known for its embrace of virtually all of the world's great religions.

The political realists often say that Gandhi's ideas and ideals have been proven naïve in the *real politik* of present-day India. Gandhi's glossy picture appears in every schoolroom and his bronze statue, striding along with his walking stick, is garlanded in every public square. Despite the adulation, India has forgotten his message, so they say. In the face of such a cynical assessment, it is important to remember that the *real politik* of Gandhi's day was no less coercive and compelling than that of our own. He sounded equally idealistic in his own time. But unlike most idealists, Gandhi did not dream up his ideals in a study filled with great books. He insisted on a higher standard for human relations and human behavior and he forged and tested it in the fire of tension, violence, competition, and racisim that plagued his time as it does ours.

Gandhi's thought has special relevance for the challenge of interreligious dialogue today precisely because it is thought that emerges from and has been tested by a life of dialogue. He was not interested in the intellectual dialogue of ideas or theologies. His views on religion do not emerge from the context of philosophical thought, as do those of S. Radhakrishnan, his near contemporary, who lived at some remove from the struggle for Indian independence and the painful tragedies of the partition. Gandhi's views emerge, rather, from the crucible of action and involvement in a world where both his partners and his adversaries were Hindus, Muslims, Christians, Jews, Sikhs, Parsis, and Jains.

Gandhi's lifelong dialogue was not with reified systems of thought, but with people who embodied those religious ideas in their own lives, lived up to them, or sometimes failed to live up to them. His dialogue as a Hindu was not with something called "Christianity" or "Islam" in the abstract, but with Christians and Muslims, with whom he worked shoulder to shoulder for sixty years. It was a ceaseless dialogue that went on nearly every day of his life. The bullet that killed him, fired by one of the Hindu revivalists who was outraged that Gandhi's hand seemed perpetually outstretched to the Muslims, was but one volley in that dialogue, and not the last.

Because his was a life of dialogue, there is much we can learn about interreligious dialogue from Gandhi's experience. What follows are home-spun Gandhian guidelines that express Gandhi's understanding of religious interrelations in a world where religious plurality is not merely an inter-esting social fact, but a fact that causes confusion, doubt, tension, and even violence.

ANEKANTAVADA: THE MANY-SIDEDNESS OF TRUTH

Gandhi is proccupied with the question of Truth. In his English writing, he capitalizes the term Truth. In the Hindu tradition the Sanskrit term is *Sat*. It means "truth, reality, being." The Upanishads use the term often. In the Chandogya Upanishad (6.2.1), for instance, the sage Uddalaka begins his teaching with the words, "In the beginning, Being (*Sat*) alone existed, one without a second. . . ." This is the term which stretches through the meanings of Being, Reality, and Truth. It also spans the meanings symbol-ized in the West by the term God. "Of late, instead of saying 'God is Truth,' I have been saying 'Truth is God,' in order to more fully define my Religion. Denial of God we have known. Denial of Truth we have not known."[1] For those who use the language of God, *Sat* might best be understood in the abstract God-language of Tillich—Ultimate Reality, Ground of Being.

Truth is many-sided. It is apprehended from many perspectives. The term *anekantavada* is used by the Jain philosophical tradition, which Gan-dhi knew, to describe the fragmentariness, the partiality, of any one view of truth. The term means, literally, "no one view is to be taken, exclusively, by itself." Truth is transcendent. Truth, or "God" if we like, always exceeds and stretches beyond our understanding of it. No one owns it all. No one can claim to have seen it all. Ultimate Reality so defies encirclement by the human mind that Hindus, like people in many religious traditions, have sometimes said that we can best approach it not by heaping up adjectives and names, but by stripping them all away. As the Brihadaranyaka Upan-ishad (2.3.6) puts it, the supreme teaching about the Real is "Neti, neti . . . Not this, not this." There are, in fact, but three words used in the Upani-shads to describe the one called Brahman. *Sat* is the first. The others are *chid*, consciousness, and *ananda*, bliss.

There is very little one can say of the Transcendent, but one thing is certain: it transcends. It transcends any one claim upon it. God is greater than our human understanding of God. Truth is fuller than our understand-ing of Truth. In encountering the religious visions and insights of people of other traditions, Gandhi begins with what, to him, is self-evident: that the Reality toward which all point passes human understanding. Indeed, one sure sign that one is losing track of Truth is the claim that one's own group has an exclusive claim upon it. "Revelation is the exclusive property of no nation, no tribe."[2]

It seems a simple insight, but the world in which we live, and in which

Gandhi lived as well, resounds with competing, exclusivist religious claims. How does a Muslim understand the religious faith of a Christian? How does a Christian understand the prayer and devotion of a Hindu? These are questions that people of every tradition of faith face today, as we become increasingly aware of the faith of our neighbors. And within each of our traditions there is, finally, the recognition of the limitations of our own religious language in apprehending the Ultimate Reality. Hindus speak of Brahman, of *Sat*, that in the face of which "mind and speech fall back, having no hold" (Taittiriya Upanishad 2.4.9). Muslims, in their daily prayers, say, *"Allahu Akbar."* Not simply, "God is great," but "God is greater." Greater than the images, names, adjectives we might be tempted to apply to God. Christians speak of the mystery of the Holy Trinity which suggests, but does not circumscribe or limit, the infinite and the intimate presence of God.

Gandhi was convinced that Truth, precisely because its claim upon us is ultimate, is many-sided and must be seen from many perspectives. There are many voices and legitimate perspectives in a complex household. There are many households in a village. There are many households of faith and ideology in the world village. There are many faces of the divine. Dialogue must begin, then, with some measure of humility in the face of the mystery of the Transcendent, however we understand it, and with some acknowledgment that others have glimpsed a part of it as well.

"ALL RELIGIONS ARE TRUE"

"I believe in Sarvadharmasamanvatva — *having equal regard for all faiths and creeds."*[3]

Gandhi's insistence on "equal regard for all religions" emerged from a distinctively Indian context. In Gujarat, where he grew up, Vaishnava Hindus and Jains lived side by side, sharing many forms of religiousness. The Pranami Vaishava tradition to which Gandhi's mother belonged used the Qur'an as well as the Bhagavad Gita in daily devotions. In such a climate it was not difficult for Hindus such as Gandhi to extend their appreciation of the many faces of the divine to include the faces shown us in other traditions. It was a painful memory of his teenage years to have heard a Christian missionary in Rajkot heaping abuse upon the gods of the Hindu tradition.

Gandhi often puts the point provocatively: "All religions are true." He uses images that are common stock in the Hindu tradition. Religions are like the many branches of the same tree, the many flowers of the one field, the many siblings of one family. Along the roads of different religious traditions, humankind travels toward a common destination. Why should we all travel the same road? Do they not converge at our destination?

Equal regard grows from the sympathetic knowledge that others experience a sense of community, inspiration, and vision from their own religious traditions that must be analogous to what we ourselves experience. The imaginative capacity to appreciate a reality that we do not share is what makes us human. Having equal regard for other religions does not mean adopting the other religion. It does, however, "compel me to understand their viewpoint, to appreciate the light in which they look upon their religion."[4]

An "equal regard" for all religions does not mean the syncretism of religions. Far from it. "I do not aim at any fusion," said Gandhi.[5] The variety of the branches, the flowers, the landscapes that our different roads enable us to see, is precisely the point. There should be no religious melting pot in which all become one. There can be no appreciation of the "other" that is premised on the hope of fusion with the other, the elimination of otherness. Appreciation of another tradition is premised on our difference, and on the faith that difference does not finally condemn us to division and enmity.

In general, Gandhi took seriously the claim of people in various religious traditions that their scriptures are revealed. His way of putting it is that they are "divinely inspired . . . but this does not oblige one to accept every single verse as divinely inspired."[6] He is very much against a literalist interpretation of scripture, however. We must use our reason to understand what the words of scripture mean to us. If the Laws of Manu insist on the subordination of woman to man, then, according to Gandhi, this aspect of the Laws of Manu is in error.

If there is indeed divine "inspiration" in the various scriptures of humankind, it should follow that these scriptures have divine gifts and inspiration to offer beyond the putative borders of the tradition which claims them as its own. An expression of Gandhi's regard for all religions was his reverent study of their scriptures. Even though our first task is to find out what these inspired writings mean to their devotees, we discover that they also mean something to us. Gandhi was interested in knowing what the New Testament means to Christians, but he was adamant about the fact that its meaning is not confined to Christians. The New Testament meant something to him, as a Hindu.

ALL RELIGIONS ARE IMPERFECT

"All faiths constitute a revelation of Truth, but all are imperfect and liable to error. Reverence for other faiths need not blind us to their faults."[7]

Religions are not revealed full-blown from heaven. They are human responses to the glimpses of God's revelation, human creations, bearing the imprint of inevitable human imperfection. Religions are not "the Truth," though they aim us toward the Truth. They are our ways of being, our paths of seeking, our communities of familial bonding, and they should not be reified into systems that are ends in themselves. Furthermore, despite their sublime ideals, all religions have had and continue to have their distortions, their times of darkness, violence, and fanaticism. The assertion of the complete superiority of one religion over another will not, in Gandhi's view, stand up to the scrutiny of history and of reason. People in all religions have fallen short of their ideals, and the religious symbols of all traditions have been twisted and misused in the name of tyranny and oppression.

Understanding requires that we glimpse the beauty of other religious traditions. After all, the major religious traditions of humankind have generated great cultures, inspired devotion, art, and music, and sustained human lives in joy and pain through many, many centuries. Each tradition has immense creative power and beauty. And yet the quest for truth reveals the darkness of all religious traditions, as well. Above all, the search for truth in dialogue requires the honesty of not comparing what is beautiful in our own tradition with what is darkest in the traditions of our neighbors.

"EXPERIMENTS" WITH TRUTH

Truth, in Gandhi's view, is not a non-negotiable dogma or principle with which he begins but a goal which he seeks. He seeks it "experimentally," as he puts it, in the experience and struggles of life. If we want to know whether the injunction, "Love your enemies," has some truth in it, we must try it out. Only in the laboratory of experience can we test our understanding of truth. Gandhi called his autobiography *The Story of My Experiments with Truth*. He meant just that: Truth is experimental, not theoretical. Experiments are proven true by testing them. So are religious convictions.

Gandhi was a vegetarian from childhood. In his didactic recollections of his teenage years, however, he recalls sneaking off with a friend to eat mutton like the Englishmen. All night he suffered from dreams of goats leaping in his stomach. He became just a bit more confirmed as a vegetarian. Still, it was a matter of uncertainty as he went off to England to study law. He was warned on the boat that he would certainly need to eat meat in England to survive the climate. At first, he kept to vegetarianism simply because he had made a vow to his mother to do so. Gradually, however, he became "intellectually converted" to vegetarianism through the writings and the company of English vegetarians. Far from being a trivial example of his experimental approach to truth, his "conversion" to the simplicity and restraint of a vegetarian diet became one of the foundations of his political philosophy.

Gandhi's political career was one based on making our religious and political ideals into the realities of our own daily lives. Gandhi was not simply opposed to untouchability: he cleaned his own latrines and adopted an untouchable child. He was not simply an advocate for the poor and a liberation theologian before his time: he took on the simplicity of the life of the poor. He did not simply respect Islam: he read the Qur'an daily as part of his own devotional life. The day before he was assasinated by a Hindu extremist, he visited a Muslim saint's shrine in the outskirts of Delhi as an act of penitence for the communal violence that had torn through the streets of the city.

For too many people, religion is a matter of ideas and principles. It is easier, somehow, to advertise them and defend them in debate than to put them into action in daily life, to test them and see how they wear, and to allow them to transform us if they wear well. Gandhi reminds us that to our encounters today with people of other traditions of faith we bring not only what we "believe," but who we are. The ideals of religious truth that we bring into dialogue with others cannot be mere ideas to which we adhere theoretically; they must be tried on and tried out in the struggles of our lives.

Every tradition affirms this in one way or another. As the Buddha put it, "Come and see, *ehi passika*." Don't simply accept religious truths. Above all, don't vaunt and brandish them. But come, look, experience, and see for yourself if they are true. As Gandhi put it, "I am convinced, I know, that God will ask, asks us now, not what we label ourselves, but what we are, i.e. what we do. With Him *deed* is everything; *belief* without deed is nothing."[8]

AHIMSA AS THE WAY TO TRUTH

"Truth is my religion and Ahimsa is the only way of its realization."[9]

If all religions are paths toward truth, then are all these paths equally good? What about the path of the Nazis? The Ku Klux Klan? Are there no criteria for valuing or privileging one path over another? These are the kinds of questions that are asked over and over, especially by those who fear that openness to dialogue implies a kind of amoral relativism. Gandhi is very clear on this question. He is not at all a moral relativist. To be open to all religions does not mean to abdicate one's judgement and throw away criteria for judgement. The plumbline for discernment is non-violence, *ahimsa*. Only through non-violence can truth be known.

"Trying on" one's own understanding of truth, wearing it day by day, living by it and in terms of it, one may become increasingly convinced of its durability. In conflict, one would hold fast to such truth, and that is the meaning of the term *satyagraha*, literally "holding on to truth." It is not "passive resistance," but an active standing up for truth, holding it fast. In the end, we might suffer and even die for our understanding of truth. But one thing we cannot do: we cannot kill for it. Gandhi speaks of "the art of dying without killing in defense of what we hold dear."[10]

Truth is incompatible with violence. This is at the heart of Gandhian nonviolent resistance and action. If Truth is, finally, transcendent, no human being has a privileged point of view above the limitations of human knowledge from which to arrogate to himself or herself the right to kill another human being for his or her view of truth. Violence closes the case and silences the voice of the other.

Violence is not only killing another. Coercion is violence. The abuse of power is violence. The willful denigration of another is violence. Violence can never shore up Truth. It can only undermine Truth. My own view of Truth does not shine more brilliantly by denigrating the views of my neighbor. It is, rather, tarnished. I do not stand taller by abusing or humiliating my neighbor, or by heaping contempt upon my neighbor's understanding of God or ways of worship. Because Truth is many-sided and transcendent, human religiousness does not fall within the economy of the "limited-good," in which the rise of one must necessitate the decline of another, the insight of one, the blindness of another.

"FRIENDLY STUDY OF THE WORLD'S RELIGIONS"

It is easy to settle for religious stereotypes. Gandhi as a young man heard the unflattering description of Hindus as idolators and polytheists in the bombastic preaching of the Christian missionaries of Rajkot. In turn, the young Gandhi heard equally distorted and stereotypical views of Christians, who were seen as propounding a "gospel" of rancor. They were called "beef and beer Christians" because Hindus identified Christians by their habits, drinking alcohol and eating beef, both of which they found repugnant. Gandhi did not settle for stereotypes, however, and did not match the missionaries' distortions of Hindus with equally distorted views of Christians. He read the Bible for himself, beginning with Genesis and reading all the way through in a disarmingly straightforward way. He admits that he found parts of it slow going and contrary to his own sensibilities, but he found the gospels profoundly compelling.

Gandhi wrote, "I hold that it is the duty of every cultured man or woman to read sympathetically the scriptures of the world. If we are to respect others' religions as we would have them to respect our own, a friendly study of the world's religions is a sacred duty."[11] "Friendly study" of the world's religions, while it is not uncritical study, does involve us in the attempt to understand another tradition from the standpoint of those who find it nourishing and challenging. For Gandhi, as a Hindu, it meant asking why it is that the Muslim or the Christian tradition has anchored the lives and grounded the affections of so many millions of people through so many hundreds of years. What is the truth in each tradition? It is easy enough to find fault with the other, even to demonize the other. More challenging is the task of understanding the beauty and the compelling truth of the other.

Friendly study means that one should study other traditions through the writings of those who are adherents of them. As Gandhi puts it, "There is one rule ... which should always be kept in mind while studying all great religions, and that is that one should study them only through the writings of known votaries of the respective religions. For instance, if one wants to study the Bhagavat, one should do so not through a translation of it made by a hostile critic, but one prepared by a lover of the Bhagavat."[12] The interdependence of the modern worlds challenges people everywhere to the serious study of religious traditions other than their own. How to do so is a critical question.

People of many religious traditions, especially in parts of the world that have known Western colonial subjugation, are very skeptical about being known primarily through the eyes of Western interpreters. Today Western interpreters are not easily written off as "hostile critics," and I, for one, would not make the case that one should study a tradition "only through the writings of known votaries." Even so, the voices and interpretations of adherents must be at the center of study. And no tradition speaks with a single voice. The very process of dialogue is multivocal.

During his years in England and South Africa, Gandhi went often to church meetings and gave Christians every opportunity to convey, in their words and lives, the meaning of the Christian faith. Interestingly, even when Christians did not convey their faith well, in Gandhi's view, he kept other Christian voices in mind. Of the racially exclusive white church in South Africa, he asked, "Is this really Christianity?" Feeling deeply that it contradicted the spirit of Jesus and the Sermon on the Mount, he concluded that it was not. On another occasion he said more broadly, "much of what passes for Christianity is a negation of the Sermon on the Mount."[13] He might be faulted for insisting on an ideal vision of Christianity, but it was a fault he shared with many Christians, including his close friend C. F. Andrews.

The "friendly study" of humankind's religions does not, in fact, reveal that they are "all the same." They are as different as families and cultures are different. Understanding the particularities and distinctive differences of each tradition is as important as understanding their similarities. As W. C. Smith has put it, "the most important thing that two religious communities can have in common is a clear and mutually agreed awareness of their differences."[14]

DEEPER UNDERSTANDING OF OUR OWN FAITH

"Cultivation of tolerance for other faiths will impart to us a truer understanding of our own."[15]

Some skeptics assume that appreciation of another religious tradition must diminish and dilute faithfulness to one's own. Gandhi is clear on this matter: "Let no one, even for a moment, entertain the fear that a reverent study of other religions is likely to weaken or shake one's faith in one's own.[16] He gave the example of his own study of Christianity. "I shall say to the Hindus that your lives will be incomplete unless you reverently study the teachings of Jesus. I have come to the conclusion, in my own experience, that those who, no matter to what faith they belong, reverently study the teachings of other faiths, broaden their own instead of narrowing their hearts.[17]

This also is not a matter of theory. Gandhi's windows and doors were always open. He wrote, "I do not want my house to be walled in on all sides and my windows and doors to be stuffed. I want the cultures of all lands to be blown about my house as freely as possible. Mine is not a religion of the prison-house." Specifically, he learned a great deal from Christians, from C. F. Andrews to Leo Tolstoy. He was profoundly moved by the Gospels, especially the Sermon on the Mount. Yet Christians could not somehow believe that this man with such an affinity for Christian ethics, such a love of Christian hymns, with such an openness to Christian friends, could appreciate all this while yet remaining a Hindu with faith and confidence in his own tradition. As Vincent Sheehan is said to have put it, "The most Christlike man in history was not a Christian at all." By his own confession, Gandhi said of Jesus, "He affects my life no less because I regard him as one among the many begotten sons of God."[18]

Gandhi used "love-language" in describing his affection for Hinduism. He meant that we love our own traditions of faith with the kind of faithful, focussed, and forgiving love that we have for our spouse. Gandhi put it this way: "I can no more describe my feeling for Hinduism than for my own wife. She moves me as no other woman in the world can. Not that she has no fault. I daresay she has many more than I see myself. But the feeling of an indissoluble bond is there."[19] Knowledge that there are other women and appreciation of their beauties does not change the primary quality of that indissoluble bond. Similarly, knowledge and appreciation of other families does not dilute our rootedness in our own, but rather enables us to see that the quality of relatedness that so grounds us in a community of loved ones is a widely shared human quality.

Many who have lived lives of interreligious dialogue affirm that the more they come to know people of other faiths, the deeper they understand and affirm their own. As one group put it, at the close of a week of dialogue, "Not only do we need to understand one another, we need one another in order to understand ourselves."[20] It is the sense that we are continually enriched by our neighbors that made Gandhi deeply appreciative, even of those with whom he disagreed most. Being able to understand the viewpoint of another gives us an invaluable gift: another place to stand from which to view ourselves.

REAL CONVERSION

"My constant prayer, therefore, is for a Christian or Muslim to be a better Christian and a better Muslim. This, to me, is real conversion."[21]

After his first distasteful impression of the Christian missionaries of Rajkot, Gandhi had some very good friends through the course of his life who were missionaries. Nonetheless, he disapproved of the proselytizing effort to convert Hindus to Christianity. Convincing people to switch over from one religion to another he saw as both mischievous and profitless, and often coercive. Furthermore, it was based on poor theology. Conversion, after all, is God's business, not ours. The missionary language of "bringing God" to the heathen or of "converting" someone to Christianity is language of sheer human hubris. God precedes the missionary to even the remotest corner of the earth, and as the for conversion of the heart, that is the work of God alone. As Gandhi put it, "I do not believe in conversion by human agency. . . . If conversion is the work of God, why should that work be taken away from him?"

Gandhi's views of proselytizing and conversion must be understood in the politicized context of conversion in India. "It is impossible for me to reconcile myself to the idea of conversion after the style that goes on in India and elsewhere today," he wrote.[22] Christian missions in India came hand in hand with the exploitative powers of empire. Before the British, the sequence of Muslim empires of India had brought with them Islamic mission. In the 1920s there were Hindu efforts, spearheaded by the revivalist Arya Samaj, to reconvert, literally purify (*shuddhi*) those who had previously converted to Islam, even centuries earlier. Thus, Gandhi's discussion of conversion was directed against all forms of conversion. "I am against conversion, whether it is known as Shuddhi by Hindus, Tabligh by Muslims, or proselytizing by Christians. Conversion is a heart-process known only to and by God."[23]

Conversion is also based on what, to Gandhi, was the untenable view of the superiority of one religion over another. "It is unthinkable that one will become good or attain salvation only if he embraces a particular religion — Hinduism, Christianity, or Islam. Purity of character and salvation depend on the purity of heart."[24] And again, "It would be the height of intolerance — and intolerance is a species of violence — to believe that your religion is superior to others' religions and that you would be justified in wanting others to change over to your faith."[25]

In one respect, however, Gandhi attached a positive meaning to the term conversion. The aim of *satyagraha* is indeed to "convert" the opponent, not to defeat the opponent. In the win-lose ethos of victory and defeat, even the winner is still left with an enemy, albeit a defeated enemy. The purpose of *satyagraha* is to convert the enemy into a friend. In a situation of conflict, active non-violent resistence is aimed not at bringing the opponent to submission, but awakening in the opponent a glimpse of truth, which one holds onto, as a *satyagrahi*, not with a closed fist, as if it were a private possession, but with the open hand of steadfast love, as if it were a gift offered freely to the opponent. In such an encounter between people with two opposing views of truth, or between people of two different religious traditions, the aim is not to convert the other to a new doctrine, but to convert the relationship from one of enmity to one of trust, even of love. That is the conversion on which Gandhi staked his life.

Because of his lack of dogma, Gandhi's style is one of openness to change, in the sense of conversion to deeper truth perceived by both sides. He did, in fact, change his mind and modify his views. He did not maintain his views as an ideology. He knew full well that only by being open to change himself could his opponents be free to change. Therefore his understanding of truth in any situation or conflict was not one he held tightly, but openly so that it could claim the allegiance of his opponent as well.

RELIGION: "THAT WHICH BINDS"

Gandhi wrote, "Religions are not for separating men from one another, they are meant to bring them together. It is a misfortune that today they are so distorted that they have become a potent cause of strife and mutual slaughter."[26] Perhaps the most critical question for which we all are accountable is "Who do we mean when we say 'we'?" Is it we Harrises, we Italian-Americans, we Methodists, we Sri Lankans, we Christians, we Muslims, or we human beings? What is the "we" that matters most to us? In terms of what "we" do we make critical decisions?

Gandhi's leadership was fundamentally based on the principle of inclusion. His ashram family and his co-workers in *satyagraha* included women and men, young and old, Muslim, Hindu, Christian and Jew, brahmins and untouchables. His house was, indeed, one in which the windows and doors were open to people of good will, regardless of faith, race, caste, or class. The exclusivism of the "prison-house" religious mentality was not only unacceptable spiritually, but was totally unviable as the basis for a new Indian community. The tragedy of India's partition did not diminish the credibility of his vision, but rather made the need for such an inclusive sense of household ever more urgent, ever more plain.

Erik Erikson, like Gandhi, has long seen the problem of what he calls "pseudo-speciation," that peculiar human tendency to identify ourselves with artificially constructed groups, castes, tribes, and nations and to see all "others" as aliens. Such pseudo-speciation is especially virulent in the religious communalism and ethnic chauvinism that seems to know no bounds today. For Erikson, and Gandhi as well, the critical question today is whether we human beings will finally choose the chauvinism of a narrow regional, ethnic, national, or religious group or the open household, ready to include, in relationship and connection, an ever larger family of humankind.

We might think that the natural human choice would be to put one's kin and family first in all decision-making. Gandhi did not quarrel with that choice, but he consistently extended and expanded what he meant by "family" to include everyone in the ashram, then every one in the village, the whole of India, and finally the whole human race. The point was to make the global decisions we make as if they were decisions affecting our closest family, for they are.

Religio means "to bind," but if those "bound together" by religion are only the people of that religion, then it is easy for religious kinship to become communal chauvinism. In Gandhi's view, the strength of kinship generated by religious bonds should not halt at the boundaries of one's own religion, but should enable people to reach out for the hands of others as well. Speaking of the dark days of communal strife that followed the partition of India, Gandhi said "I am striving to become the best cement between the two communities. My longing is to be able to cement the two with my blood, if necessary. But, before I can do so, I must prove to the Muslims that I love them as well as I love the Hindus."[27]

Bonding between human beings was at the basis of Gandhi's style of social action, for he was certain that a situation of enmity will not change in the absence of a transformed relationship. Relationship requires the stockpiling of trust and good will. Even when relationship has been betrayed, Gandhi insists that one reach out to the opponent and trust again. Finally, one is trusting the inner truth that is in every human being. For example, Gandhi, imprisoned by Jan Smuts in South Africa, made Smuts a pair of leather sandals in prison and presented them to him on his release. Reaching out to a new relationship with an opponent was integral to Gandhi's style of leadership. Gandhi also corresponded with his opponents, as in his famous letter to Lord Irwin, the Viceroy of India, which he wrote before undertaking the Salt March. It is a letter in which he begs Irwin to change his mind about the salt tax, which unjustly affects the poorest of the poor. He reminds the Viceroy that his salary is 5000 times that of the average Indian. Granting that the Viceroy "probably donates the whole of it to charity," he nevertheless insists that a system which permits such inequity should be "summarily scrapped." He closes, "Your friend, M. K. Gandhi."

YOUR FRIEND, M. K. GANDHI

These simple words summarize as well as any the guidelines for inter-religious encounter one might find in Gandhi's thought. Let us return once again to the beginning of this essay: dialogue is with people, more than with systems of thought. Gandhi reminds us that in the encounter with the "other," whether an opponent in political controversy or a person of a very different faith or culture from one's own, there is always a person on both sides of the encounter. Gandhi's style of relationship and dialogue, therefore, was personalist, premised on the invariable fact that every controversy and encounter involves human beings, not just positions or abstract convictions.

Gandhi himself was not a giant. Indeed, what was most charismatic about him was not the charisma of superhumanity, but an endearing, recognizable, humanity, reduced by the leanness of his dress and possessions, to the bare basics. Gandhi did not accept a "role" —the strategist, the reformer, the politician, the Mahatma. He was a person. He was a person who did not hide the fact that he thought about and struggled with decisions. He was a person who said so when a campaign had been a dreadful mistake. He called one decision a "Himalayan miscalculation." Because he did not play a role, but rather had a "sense of himself" he could act with a tremendous sense of freedom.

On his side of the relationship, Gandhi was a real person, with no posturing in him. He was free to be open, free to change his mind, free to compromise if necessary, and free to die if necessary. On the other side of the relationship of enmity or confrontation, Gandhi left room for a real person as well—a person for whom he stitched leather sandals, a person to whom he addressed a personal letter, a person who might be moved by the open hand of friendship or by a word of love.

The lessons of *satyagraha* for interreligious encounter are important. These encounters are, first and foremost, encounters of persons with differing views of truth. To attempt to understand the religious viewpoint of someone of another faith is one of the greatest challenges of human mind and heart, as is the challenge to be understood by the other. It is not enough to understand an idea or a concept from another worldview, but we must glimpse how a multitude of ideas and concepts, symbols and stories, images and songs, festivals and rites, compose an entire world of meaning, and we must at least be able to imagine moving into that world and living in terms of it. We must be able to glimpse what truth looks like from that standpoint. Difficult as it may seem, it is also no less than what we ask of others in their understanding of ourselves.

Understanding is a mutual trust. The openness in dialogue to the truth as glimpsed by the other may appear threatening to some, but we can do no less if we are to elicit in the "other" an openness to the truth as we see it. If it is a risk for Christians to try to understand the faith of a Muslim or Hindu through dialogue, it is no less a risk for the Muslim or Hindu to try to understand the faith of a Christian. We are responsible for the image of one another. If Christians distort the image of the Hindu or Muslim through a misrepresentation of their faith, so equally might Hindus or Muslims distort the image of the Christian. We both have a stake in a deepening dialogue that rectifies our mutual understanding and leads us to mutual conversion.

NOTES

1. M. K. Gandhi, *All Religions are True*, edited by Anand T. Hingorani (Bombay: Bharatiya Vidya Bhavan, 1962), p. 231. This book contains an edited collection of Gandhi's writings on religion, primarily from his two publications, *Harijan* and

Young India, from 1920 to 1947. Unfortunately, they are woven together so seamlessly in this volume that it is difficult to contextualize any part of the text.

2. *All Religions are True*, p. 25.

3. *All Religions are True*, p. 7.

4. *All Religions are True*, p. 7.

5. *All Religions are True*, p. 8.

6. *All Religions are True*, p. 8

7. *All Religions are True*, p. 2

8. *All Religions are True*, p. 59.

9. *All Religions are True*, p. 233.

10. *Harijan*, March 6, 1937.

11. *Young India*, September 2, 1926.

12. *All Religions are True*, p. 22.

13. C. F. Andrews, *Mahatma Gandhi's Ideas, Including Selections from his Writings*. (New York: The Macmillan Press), 1930, p. 94. The entire chapter "The Place of Jesus" addresses this question.

14. W. C. Smith, *Religious Diversity*, (New York: Crossroad, 1982) p. 113.

15. *All Religions are True*, p. 3.

16. *All Religions are True*, p. 22.

17. *All Religions are True*, p. 51.

18. *All Religions are True*, p. 60.

19. *All Religions are True*, p. 137.

20. World Council of Churches, Statement from the Mauritius Multilateral Dialogue on "The Meaning of 'Life.' "

21. *All Religions are True*, p. 59, 234.

22. *All Religions are True*, p. 44.

23. *All Religions are True*, p. 43.

24. *All Religions are True*, p. 40.

25. *All Religions are True*, p. 225.

26. *All Religions are True*, p. 228.

27. M. K. Gandhi, *The Way to Communal Harmony* (Ahmedchad: Navajivan Publishing House), p. 5.

——— Chapter Six ———

Gandhi's Way of the Cross

Ignatius Jesudasan, S. J.

Ignatius Jesudasan is an Indian Jesuit who received his doctorate at Marquette University. Currently he lives in Tamilnadu, where he is director of the Gandhian Society Villages Association, an organization which he organized to promote village development. The selection which follows is taken from his book, *A Gandhian Theology of Liberation* (Orbis Books, 1984).

GANDHIAN CHRISTOLOGY

Christology can be seen from two points of view—as description or as prescription. For Gandhi, the descriptive aspect, which takes the form of worship and dogma, is subservient to the prescriptive aspect, which consists of imitation of Christ or moral identification with him as manifesting the underlying truth of the spiritual unity of all humankind. Gandhi saw Christ as an ideal *satyagrahi.*

Gandhi's Christology can be discovered in the context of the Christian concept of service to one's fellow humans, which was a guiding principle of his life. Gandhi's search through *satyagraha* was not for his own salvation, but for communal growth in truth, involving whole races and peoples converging in mutual recognition and love. As James Douglass points out:

When God is sought as truth, God draws the seekers into a growing community of love. The concrete way in which Gandhi suffered toward this community of seeking men is the point at which his experiments coincide most perfectly with the life and death of Christ.[1]

According to Douglass, the significance of Gandhi can be seen in the authentically Christian terms of a socially and politically active suffering love. (Gandhi once wrote: "To me God is Truth and love. . . . He is long-suffering.")

A Christology inspired by the spirit or self-understanding of Jesus, as that self-understanding is appropriated in faith, must recognize in Gandhi's discipleship to—and imitation of—truth or self-sacrificing love, an eminent example of what Karl Rahner terms "anonymous Christianity." Gandhi's own self-understanding, as dedicated to truth and self-sacrificing love, implicitly reproduces a central aspect of Jesus' own self-understanding. In other words, the Hindu Gandhi fulfilled in his life the injunction of St. Paul to the Christians of Philippi: "In your minds you must be the same as Christ Jesus" (Phil. 2:5). It is noteworthy in this connection that the popular association of Gandhi in India was not so much with the great names in the world's political history, but with the great names in the religious history of the world. As influential as he was in shaping the political history of the country, Gandhi was looked upon primarily as a man of faith.

GANDHI'S VIEW OF CHRIST

Gandhi's view of Christ does not reinforce Christian dogma, but goes beyond dogma to embrace Christian morality. From his youth, Gandhi had evaluated the *Vedas* and the *Upanishads* on the basis of their ethical or practical teachings. Miracles had no interest for him as apology or proof. Upon his first reading of the Bible he was repelled by the literal meaning of many biblical texts, refusing to take them as the Word of God. In evaluating all Scriptures, his criterion was morality—not sectarian, but universal morality. If religions gave conflicting counsel, Gandhi applied three criteria by which to discriminate among them: (1) the superiority of truth over everything that conflicted with it; (2) rejection of everything that conflicted with nonviolence; and (3) on things that could be reasoned out, rejection of everything that conflicted with reason.[2] Thus that which reconciled Gandhi to any teaching of Jesus was not his alleged miracles, but the conformity of his teaching with Gandhi's criteria of universal morality.

In this light, Jesus was to Gandhi a great world-teacher among others: "He was to the devotees of his generation no doubt the only begotten son of God."[3] For Gandhi, however, to believe that Jesus was the "only begotten son of God" was contrary to reason; the word "son" therefore can be used only in a figurative sense. Gandhi claimed that the adjective "begotten" had for him "a deeper and possibly a grander meaning than its literal meaning. " It implied "spiritual birth. In his own times he [Jesus] was the nearest to God."[4] In this sense any person with the qualities of Jesus is a begotten son of God: "If a man is spiritually miles ahead of us we may say that he is in a special sense the son of God, though we are all children of God. We repudiate the relationship in our lives, whereas his life is a witness to that relationship."[5] Jesus affected Gandhi's life no less because he regarded him as one among the many begotten sons of God. For Gandhi, Jesus was "as divine as Krishna or Rama or Mahomed or Zoroaster."[6]

Gandhi believed that Jesus had attained the highest degree of perfection possible for a person, given the limitations of the flesh. He discounted miracles for much the same theological reasons as Rudolf Bultmann would at a later date, namely, the actual negation of the divine transcendence involved in the conception, despite every intent to affirm that transcendence. Gandhi wrote:

> I believe in the perfectibility of human nature. Jesus came as near to perfection as possible. To say that he was perfect is to deny God's superiority to man. And then in this matter I have a theory of my own. Being necessarily limited by the bonds of flesh, we can attain perfection only after dissolution of the body. Therefore God alone is absolutely perfect. When He descends to earth, He of His own accord limits Himself. Jesus died on the Cross because he was limited by the flesh. I do not need either the prophecies or the miracles to establish Jesus's greatness as a teacher. Nothing can be more miraculous than the three years of his ministry. . . . I do not deny that Jesus had certain psychic powers and he was undoubtedly filled with the love of humanity. . . . But he brought to life not people who were dead but who were believed to be dead. The laws of Nature are changeless, unchangeable, and there are no miracles in the sense of infringement or interruption of Nature's laws. But we limited beings fancy all kinds of things and impute our limitations to God. We may copy God, but not He us.[7]

Gandhi is affirming the perfection of Jesus at the moment of his death rather than locating it at any one moment or even within the total duration of his life. Gandhi associates perfection with the resurrection and relates worship to the perfection seen by the eyes of believers. Thus, asked about the worship of "incarnations" who were historical figures, he said:

> Christians worship the Christ who was resurrected. In the same manner those who worship Rama and Krishna worship Rama and Krishna who are more living than you are, or certainly more living than I am. They live now and will live until eternity. . . . I worship the living Rama and Krishna, the incarnation of all that is True and Good and Perfect.[8]

Gandhi believed in the pluralism of religions as reflecting God's will to save all. He distrusted dogma, and believed in the essential equality of religions. Equality of religions meant that each religion provided truth to its respective adherents in their beliefs, gave them a framework in which to relate to God, and provided them with moral standards. All religions are divine in their inspiration, though equally imperfect in that they are received and transmitted by human instruments. Different religions are therefore beautiful flowers from the same garden; or they are branches of the same majestic tree. Hence they are equally true. They are also equal in their capacity to grow.

This same argument of equality applies to the personages of the various religions. Thus the prophets within the Bible—Moses and Jesus, for example—are equal on the "historical plane." He acknowledged the Christ of C. F. Andrews, who was not the Christ of "a narrow sect, but the Anointed of humanity, whom he sees in Ramakrishna, Chaitanya, and many other teachers of other faiths."[9]

Gandhi located himself and his nonviolence within the great tradition of nonviolence, which he traced from the Buddha through Christ even to Muhammad. He saw it as his duty to enrich this tradition. The burden of the tradition was not just an individual mission, but a collective tradition. Refuting an article in *The Statesman*, which said that the example of Jesus proved the definitive failure of nonviolence in the worldly sense, Gandhi replied:

> Though I cannot claim to be a Christian in the sectarian sense, the example of Jesus' suffering is a factor in the composition of my undying faith in non-violence which rules all my actions, worldly and temporal. And I know that there are hundreds of Christians who believe likewise. Jesus lived and died in vain if he did not teach us to regulate the whole of life by the eternal Law of Love.[10]

It was Gandhi's conviction that the root of the evil of violence was the want of a living faith in a living God. He considered it a tragedy that peoples of the earth who claimed to believe in the message of Jesus, whom they described as the Prince of Peace, showed little of that belief in actual practice. It pained him to see Christian divines limiting the scope of Jesus' message to select individuals. He wished to "convince honest doubters that the love that Jesus taught and practiced was not a mere personal virtue, but that it was essentially a social and collective virtue."[11]

Gandhi's feeling was that most Christians tended to reject the moral substance of Christ's teaching for the metaphysical symbols embodied in dogmas or creedal formulas. If the morals of a person were a matter of no concern, the particular form of worship in a church, mosque, or temple was not only an empty formula but might even be a hindrance to individual or social growth. And insistence on a particular form or repetition of a credo might be a potential cause of violent quarrels, which would have the effect of discrediting the basis of all religions, that is, belief in God. Gandhi saw Jesus' atonement, which should have been an example for imitation, flouted by many Christians in their understanding of it as a substitution, and wasted on those who did not change their lives. Rejecting such Christianity for the true message of Christ, he stated: "I rebel against orthodox Christianity, as I am convinced that it has distorted the message of Jesus. He was an Asiatic whose message was delivered through many media and when it had the backing of the Roman emperor, it became an imperialist faith as it remains to this day."[12] While Gandhi disputed the claim of Christianity to be the only true religion, he looked upon it as one of the true religions—a noble one, which along with others had contributed to raising the moral height of humankind, though it had yet to fulfill its potential in contributing to nonviolence.

GANDHI AND THE CROSS

As James Douglass has pointed out, "When the Gospel has become a fixture of culture, and thus been crowned with irrelevance, the discipline required to pass over to the standpoint of Jesus crucified must receive its inspiration from beyond that culture."[13] From that point of view, it might seem providential that Gandhi remained a Hindu despite the many and persistent attempts that had been made toward his conversion.

Douglass uses Gandhi and his interpretation of *satyagraha* for a rediscovery of the humanity of Christ and the cross as the necessary condition for a rediscovery of the divinization or lordship of Christ. The cross serves as the point of the passing from the "incarnational heresy" to the universal transcendence or inclusiveness of the incarnation as suffering love. But Douglass would seem to part company with Gandhi in stressing Christocentrism,[14] whereas Gandhi was always centered on God. For Gandhi the cross is the symbol of the theocentric rather than the Christocentric life. He dared not think of Christ's birth without his death on the cross, and could proclaim as his Christmas message: "Living Christ means a living Cross, without it life is a living death."[15]

The universality and transcendence that Gandhi recognized in Jesus was related to the universal appeal he recognized in the cross and in Jesus' Sermon on the Mount. The sermon, relating to nonretaliation and nonresistance to evil, echoed something he had learned and made a part of his being from childhood. The universality he saw in the cross was a potential universality, depending on the meaning given to the cross. Self-suffering was applicable to any individual or any nation, although Christian usage, confining it to Jesus, had failed to recognize this. For Gandhi the universality of Jesus' message was due to the power of his death, which had confirmed his [Jesus'] own word. Orthopraxis was more important, powerful, and authoritative than orthodoxy. The crucifix was to Gandhi an eloquent sermon proclaiming "that nations, like individuals, could only be made through the agony of the Cross and in no other way."[16] On the basis of this unique interpretation and application of the Sermon on the Mount, Gandhi could claim to be a Christian, unfettered by any sect or church or denomination.

Gandhi made his own meaning of the universality of the cross and of Christ when he declared, "God did not bear the Cross only 1900 years ago, but He bears it today, and He dies and is resurrected from day to day."[17]

The cross exists for all who are receptive to it. Where people are not receptive and suffering takes place in a moral vacuum, however, the suffering so suffered is itself the cross, and the dynamics of redemption can be understood in terms of *ahimsa*, or nonviolence. The dynamism of the cross is to bring the inflictor to recognize with the victim the unity of all in Christ. The dynamism of nonviolence is to move the inflictor to recognize with the victim their common humanity. To bring about this recognition of faith, suffering is necessary. The saving revelation of God takes place through the forgiving and redeeming love of the willing victim.

To affirm Gandhi's faith in Christ is not to claim Gandhi for Christianity, nor is it merely to see the full meaning of Christ through Gandhi. Through his existential identification with the God of suffering and saving love, Gandhi passes into the redeeming reality of the incarnation, opening and showing the way for us to do the same.

CHRISTIANITY AND CHRISTOLOGY

The Christian significance of Gandhi and his challenge to Christianity in India have been widely recognized. At least by the Christian missionaries and Indian Christians who formed part of his intimate circle of friends, Gandhi's importance to Christianity was appreciated while he was yet alive. From the time of his death acknowledgment of his significance has increased.

In his study of the Christian relevance of Gandhi, *The Acknowledged Christ of the Indian Renaissance*, M. M. Thomas suggests that one of the most important tasks of the church is to reconstruct the Gandhian insights about the ethics of Christ within the framework of its doctrine of redemption in Christ.[18] While admitting Gandhi's Christian significance, however, he differs with Gandhi, as many Christian theologians do, on the issue of Gandhi's emphasis on the moral life of the believer, based on the Sermon on the Mount, as opposed to the centrality of the person of Christ.

Though he emphasized the Sermon on the Mount, Gandhi never elevated ethical teaching or doctrine above faith. Through one's faith, one could commit oneself to a value enshrined in a doctrine and allow the power of that value to guide and direct one's life. Thus a life committed to value is a life of faith. Praxis is the empirical measure and criterion of faith.

Even when Gandhi speaks of the Sermon on the Mount as the whole of Christianity, he does so from the perspective of one whose life is committed to the values enshrined in that sermon. Following the example set by Jesus, Gandhi sees the essence of Christianity as a life of faith committed to the values of God and fellow humans. Jesus was more than merely an ethical teacher. The way of Jesus' values was his way to the Father, the way to establish the kingdom of God. The grace of God is the constant milieu of Gandhian ethical commitment.

Gandhi does not deny divine self-disclosure in the person and self-understanding of Jesus. What he denies is the uniqueness of that self-disclosure to Jesus. The Gandhian faith makes central the person and deeds of every believer, not merely the person of Jesus, nor merely his sermon in the abstract.

The faith with which Gandhi committed himself to the imitation of the Christ of the Sermon on the Mount transformed Gandhi into an *alter Christus*, another Christ, just as it is the faith of any Christian, and not merely the ritual of baptism, that makes him or her an *alter Christus*. Since Gandhi was not baptized he was not a "Christian." Despite this, or maybe because of it, his faith was purer and freer than that of many Christians. And the words of a believer whose faith and vision are pure provide a theological challenge for those who call themselves Christians.

That Jesus holds the central place in Christian belief is a fact that Gandhi knew and accepted as valid within the context of Christian history and the Christian community. He even accepted it as Christian testimony when it was proclaimed within the context of a Christian subjectivity. What he could not accept was the objectification of Christianity, which denied the analogous subjectivity of the non-Christian; this changed a positive, subjective testimony into an aggressive denial of salvation to those who did not assent to an objectified Christological dogma.

Gandhi was aware of the liturgical or confessional origins of creedal formulations. In the "mood of exaltation" of worship, arising from communion with the worshiped and other worshipers, every affirmation about the object of worship is equally a self-affirmation of the worshiper. It is a confession by which one's whole moral and spiritual life is regulated, and the community's life ordered. In genuine in-group cultic testimony and sharing of experience this inclusive self-affirmation is so transparent to the witness that one does not lose one's moorings in kerygma. In the objectification of belief as the absolute truth or dogma, however, making this dogma the criterion of the truth of out-group faith, the transparency of self-affirmation is lost. The testimony unwittingly becomes a conquering religio-political ideology, even if in the name of Jesus.

Gandhi challenges Christians to the Christology of Jesus as servant rather than the Christology of the church about Jesus as Lord. Gandhi does not challenge the lordship of Jesus, but the unspoken lordship of the church. He reminds us of the pedagogical function of cult, as well as the role of the cult-object as teacher. Gandhi calls us to learn the full meaning of vicarious existence from Jesus, and to apply it in our worship, belief, missionary action, and suffering.

ORTHOPRAXIS AS GANDHIAN CHRISTOLOGY

If the central issue in Gandhi's criticism of Christianity is Christology as dogma, the resolution of Gandhi's criticism is through orthopraxis, or right action. In most of the missionary practice with which Gandhi was familiar, non-Christian religions were regarded in Christian dogma as existing either in ignorance or in error. What Gandhi was opposed to, then, was not dogma, but the dogmatism of the Christian missionary evangelism of his time.

Recognizing that "... every one of us is a son of God and capable of doing what Jesus did, if we but endeavor to express the Divine in us,"[19] Gandhi drew from Christianity to transform Hinduism in at least three significant ways. First, he realized the Christic presence of God in the poor and the untouchables, initiating actions to break down the barriers that surrounded them and bring them back into the Hindu fold. Second, influenced by Christian thinking, he reinterpreted karma as a social and communal expression of sin and salvation rather than an isolated, individualized relationship with God. Third, he saw the necessity of the cross or suffering love (ahimsa) for the God-realization of all people. In each instance, Gandhi saw social and political liberation as the manifestation of these specifically Christian contributions to his transformation of Hinduism. Therein also he demonstrated the locus of his Christology in praxis or action.

Gandhian Christology is an expression of the experience of liberation based on the spirituality of a liberator who is placed beside Jesus Christ, becomes another Christ, and does not replace or displace him. In accepting the depths of human weakness, Gandhi made the power of God manifest, as Jesus had before him. In his search for truth he bridged the gap between Christian theology and Hindu spirituality. Where Max Weber had only analyzed the relationship between the Protestant ethic and the spirit of capitalism, without making any judgment upon it, and Marx had taken a committed stand for the dispossessed proletariat, but introduced a contradiction between religious faith and the process of social liberation, Gandhi resolved the contradiction by making religious faith an ally and an instrument in the social and political liberation of human beings. Social and political liberation were correlatives to spiritual liberation.

In his unflinching dedication to truth as God, in his relentless attempt to realize that truth through action and prayer, in his openness to correction and criticism, in his alignment with the poor and the voiceless, and in his suffering and death for justice sealed in fellowship and reconciliation, Gandhi can be seen as a man whose prayer, with Francis of Assisi and Ignatius of Loyola, to be placed with Christ the liberator was answered abundantly.

NOTES

1. James Douglass, *The Non-Violent Cross: A Theology of Revolution and Peace* (New York: Macmillan Company, 1970), pp. 45-46.

2. *Collected Works of Mahatma Gandhi* (New Delhi: Publications Division of the Ministry of Information and Broadcasting, Government of India), vol. 64:398. Henceforth, *CW*.

3. *CW* 62:334.

4. Ibid.

5. *CW* 64:398.

6. *CW* 64:397.

7. *Harijan*, Apr. 17, 1937; *CW* 65:82.

8. *CW* 64:420.

9. Letter to Kirby Page, Oct. 17, 1937; *CW* 66:250.

10. *Harijan*, Jan. 7, 1939; *CW* 68:278.

11. *Harijan*, Mar. 4, 1939; *CW* 62:306-7.

12. *Harijan*, May 30, 1936; *CW* 62:388.

13. James Douglass, *The Non-Violent Cross*, p. 66.

14. Ibid., p. 64.

15. M. K. Gandhi, *What Jesus Means to Me*, ed. R. K. Prabhu (Ahmedabad: Navajivan Publishing House, 1959), p. 16.

16. M. K. Gandhi, *The Message of Jesus*, ed. A. T. Hingorani (Bombay: Bharatiya Vidhya Bhavan, 1963), p. 68.

17. Ibid., pp. 37-38.

18. M. M. Thomas, *The Acknowledged Christ of the Indian Renaissance* (London: SCM Press, 1969), pp. 234-36.

19. *Harijan*, Aug. 4, 1940.

—— **Chapter Seven** ——

From Gandhi to Christ:
God as Suffering Love

James W. Douglass

James W. Douglass is a writer and long-time peace activist who has, in his many writings and experiments in nonviolent action, tried to apply Gandhian insights to the challenge of Christian discipleship. Douglass was a founder of the Ground Zero Community in Bangor, Washington, which has for many years waged a nonviolent campaign against the "White Train" shipments of nuclear weapons. The following chapter is adapted from his first book, *The Non-Violent Cross: A Theology of Revolution and Peace* (New York: Macmillan, 1968). His most recent book is *The Nonviolent Coming of God* (Orbis Books, 1991).

INCARNATIONAL HERESY

Before inquiring into Gandhi's relationship to Christ and from there into a nonviolent christology, it is necessary to consider first a phenomenon which provides a significant contrast to Gandhi's experiments in truth and which will suggest why Gandhi is so important today for an understanding of the Christian Gospel: the scandal of Western Christianity's denial of its own truth.

The truth proclaimed by Christianity is the truth of a living person. The claim of the Gospel is that God's truth has become incarnate and redemptive, has been revealed in the person and life of Jesus. Christian truth is Jesus Christ; the incarnate truth of Jesus remains present in the mystical identity between Christ and the faithful, whoever, and wherever these may be. At the center of any definition of Christian truth is therefore its nature as incarnation, a truth whose fullness is the life of Jesus and whose continuing presence is that same life as given in the Holy Spirit (but resisted by sin) in his followers.

Yet it must be admitted that such a living truth has not always been reflected in the life of Christians. Stephen Schwarzschild, a sensitive critic of Christianity, has written: "The doctrine of the Incarnation has always tempted Christians to make their peace with whatever this world has been at any given time." The form of the Incarnation Christians worship, that of humility, service, suffering love, and a sacrificial death, has seldom been matched by the cultural forms they have identified with "incarnationally." Much of the Christianity we know today can be understood and evaluated best as an incarnational heresy, which is to say, as a choice made for a theoretical faith, imbedded in a milieu consciousness, to the exclusion of the living Christic reality of suffering love. The truth of Jesus, while remaining dogmatically protected, has not become flesh in a living, suffering belief. Modern Christianity has been incarnate instead only in the wrong flesh, that of self and of the extended culture-self.

The significance of Mohandas Gandhi, for a Christianity which has capitulated to its various milieux and thus become an incarnational heresy, is that Gandhi concentrated his entire life and being on the Christic reality of suffering love. Moreover, through his experiments in truth he committed himself to suffering love in such a way that the power of Christ was demonstrated in terms of a social and political revolution. By not allying himself with Western Christianity, Gandhi kept himself independent of the incarnational heresy characteristic of it and worshipped none of the gods of established disorder. He was therefore free to reopen the way for a return to the Gospel of Peace and the revolutionary power of the cross which stands at its summit.

In view of the heresy characteristic of the West, the relationship of the Hindu Gandhi to the person of Christ can be described as one of the most living beliefs in the Incarnation given in our time, and that in full recognition of the fact that Gandhi did not confess Jesus as the only Son of God. For Gandhi had a profound sense of the suffering, loving Christ. Though he never claimed to be a Christian, Gandhi often testified to the importance of Jesus' suffering as a factor in his undying faith in nonviolence.

Gandhi rejected Christianity for the sake of Jesus. He understood and revered Christ as catholic and could not reconcile the universal meaning he saw in him with the imperialist faith he met in Christianity. In rejecting the milieu-Christianity of the West, he rejected as well the church and doctrines he associated with it. Gandhi did not accept Jesus as the only Son of God because that doctrine as presented to him by friends anxious to claim him for Christianity always struck him as too exclusive. If God could have children, all human beings were God's children. For Gandhi, "Jesus preached not a new religion, but a new life. He called men to repentance."

To define the catholic Christ of Gandhi more precisely, one can say that Gandhi committed himself to Christ morally in the Sermon on the Mount and existentially in the cross. Concerning the Sermon, which he felt "was delivered not merely to the peaceful disciples but a groaning world," Gandhi wrote: "The teaching of the Sermon on the Mount echoed something I had learnt in childhood and something which seemed to be part of my being and which I felt was being acted up to in the daily life around me . . . This teaching was non-retaliation, or non-resistance to evil."

The cross too was a reality meant for all human beings: "The Cross, undoubtedly, makes a universal appeal the moment you give it a universal meaning in place of the narrow one that is often heard at ordinary meetings." Gandhi followed Christ in identifying genuine faith and discipleship with the taking up of one's personal cross. In a talk given to a group of Christians on Christmas Day, he said: "We dare not think of birth without death on the cross. Living Christ means a living Cross; without it life is a living death."

"WHO DO YOU SAY I AM?"

As for the Christianity which Gandhi rejected, there the christological problem of our time may be posed with reference to that milieu-consciousness which has so often meant capitulation for the Christian conscience. Our christological problem would then rightly take the form of the same two questions Jesus asked the disciples in the passage that is the center of the earliest Gospel (Mark 8:27–29), with the difference that in our case we can hardly hear Jesus' decisive second question. The first, preliminary question, "Who do people say that I am?" is virtually the only one modern Christians have recognized. But it is a sociological question, one of current opinion, to which the proper answer is simply the kind of descriptive response given by the disciples in Mark: "Some say . . . Others say . . . " Yet the contemporary Christian answer to this question has been either the basis for dismissal or a substitute for faith.

On the one hand, Christians have heard this first question as "Who do *secular* people say that I am?" and have dismissed their answers as the expressions of a belligerent unbelief. On the other hand, they have heard the question as "Who do *Christians* say that I am?" and have accepted those equally milieu-given answers as the form of their own faith instead of recognizing them as the reflections of a popular religiosity. In neither case has the response to Jesus' first question served the purpose he intended, namely, to serve as the background for an altogether personal confession of faith paralleling that of Peter. As for Jesus' second and decisive question of faith, "But who do *you* say that I am?" which abruptly cuts off each disciple from the support of his or her secular-Christian milieu and confronts them with the fearful task of personal decision, the Christian of today normally does not even hear it.

In the absence of any real theological recognition of the incessant demand of Christ, "But who do you—modern disciples—say that I am?" cultural dogma has easily prevailed.

Before we can affirm the shattering truth that Jesus was God we must seek to know Jesus as fully human. To know Jesus as human is to know him in terms of that concept by which he knew himself; it is to know him as *ebed Yahweh*, the Suffering Servant of God.

The Suffering Servant of Yahweh is, first of all, a profoundly Jewish concept, rooted in the Servant poems of Isaiah and exemplified in the living history of Judaism. The primary meaning of the *ebed Yahweh* as given in Isaiah is that the Servant of God through his innocent suffering and death takes the place of the many who should suffer instead of him. The truth revealed in the *ebed Yahweh* is that salvation comes through suffering.

The beginning of Jesus' consciousness that he had to realize the task of the Suffering Servant can be traced to the moment of his baptism by John in the Jordan. The words of the voice from heaven, "Thou art my beloved Son, with thee I am well pleased," are a quotation from the opening line of the *ebed Yahweh* poems. In Isaiah these words are addressed by Yahweh to his Servant. For Jesus to have heard them spoken to him at his baptism must have compelled a recognition that he had to take on the full role of the *ebed Yahweh*, introduced in Isaiah as favored of God but destined in the unfolding drama of the poems "to pour out his soul to death."

The development of Jesus' conscious identification with the *ebed Yahweh* can be followed through the Gospel in his more and more frequent references to his suffering and death as central to the work he must accomplish. This rising sense of the *ebed*'s impending task is supported by Jesus' claim that Isaiah 53 will be fulfilled in himself. The one other concept which figures prominently in Jesus' own formulation of his work, that of the Son of Man—or, a better translation, the Human Being—is united with the theme of the Suffering Servant: "For the Human Being also came not to be served but to serve, and to give his life as a ransom for many." Although Jesus refers to himself in the Gospel as the Human Being, he nevertheless merges it with the meaning of the *ebed Yahweh* so that the vocation of the *ebed* becomes the main content of the Human Being's earthly work.

The decisive question Jesus asked of his disciples, "But who do you say that I am?" was not answered by Peter in terms of the *ebed Yahweh*. Rather, Peter's response was "You are the Christ." What is significant about this profession of faith is that Jesus wasn't satisfied with it. Not only did he go on to link his own messianic vocation to great suffering, "to teach them that the Human Being must suffer many things, and be rejected . . . and be killed," but he also sharply rebuked Peter's suggestion that such suffering was somehow avoidable: "Get behind me, Satan! For you are not on the side of God, but of human beings." Thus, suffering, rejection and a sacrificial death are essential to define the Christ. To profess a true faith in Jesus Christ is to profess a faith in Jesus the Suffering Servant.

NONVIOLENCE AND THE CROSS

At this point the words of Gandhi, "Living Christ means a living Cross; without it life is a living death," find their foundation in Jesus' statement of what it means to follow him. For a faith in Christ is not possible without the symbol and demanding reality which sums up a christocentric life: "If any would come after me, let them deny themselves and take up their cross and follow me." Though Gandhi did not claim to be a Christian, the example of Jesus' suffering was at the root of his faith in nonviolence. For him the suffering of Jesus so defined the law of Love that love and suffering were seen as one in a single flame of life. And it is thus, in terms of suffering servanthood, that Jesus defined his own vocation on earth and the vocation of any person who would travel his way.

Faith without crucifixion is meaningless. "Christianity," therefore means nothing to Christ: "Not everyone who says to me, 'Lord, Lord,' shall enter the kingdom of heaven, but whoever does the will of my Father who is in heaven."

Because the Suffering Servant is the key to Jesus' own understanding of his mission on earth, and thus the key to our understanding of his humanity, we shall be able to affirm the full truth of Jesus' humanity only by passing over the standpoint of suffering servanthood. And, as we have seen, it is only by passing through Jesus' humanity that we can feel the overwhelming mystery of his divinity. The essence of his humanity, suffering servanthood, is a reality which can hardly be understood except through an existential commitment to it as such. There can be no theoretical appropriation of the meaning of suffering as it is expressed in the *ebed Yahweh* and in Jesus.

To follow to its conclusion Mark's christological passage, we can understand Jesus' explanation of cross-bearing, "whoever loses his or her life for my sake and the gospel's will save it," as the description of an existential passing over to the standpoint of Jesus' humanity, and through the suffering love of Jesus' humanity to the overwhelming mystery of Incarnation. When the Gospel has become a fixture of culture, and thus has been crowned with irrelevance, the discipline required to pass over to the standpoint of Jesus crucified must receive its inspiration from beyond that culture. For no milieu-Christianity professes a living faith in the cross. To pass over to the standpoint of the Suffering Servant, one must learn to see with new eyes, one must be struck by the lightening of the cross.

This kind of shock was provided during the great nonviolent campaign for Indian independence in 1930–31. At one stage row upon row of unarmed and praying Hindus marched into the blows of steel lathis wielded by British-directed police. Gandhi's volunteers by the thousands walked into certain injury and possible death. Gandhi and his followers deliberately offered their bodies and their lives to the British, thus resisting them in spirit and in truth. As Indian casualties rose, British self-justification fell. India's eventual assumption of power came through blood and crucifixion, not because the British were particularly kind-hearted. To those who witnessed scenes such as those at the Dharasana salt works in 1930, where hundreds of Gandhi's followers were beaten mercilessly, the British seemed brutal enough to make the confrontation between armed might and the power of suffering love a genuine one. In any event, Gandhi's faith in nonviolent resistance was realistic enough not to rest on the presumably civilized sensibilities of the opponent or the hope of an early victory. Gandhi rooted his nonviolent faith in voluntary suffering without limit.

The logic of nonviolence is the logic of crucifixion and leads the person of nonviolence into the heart of the suffering Christ. The purpose of nonviolence is to move the oppressors to perceive those whom they are oppressing as human beings. Humans commit acts of violence and injustice against other human beings only to the extent that they do not regard them as fully human. Nonviolent resistance seeks to persuade the aggressors to recognize in their victims the humanity they have in common; when that is fully recognized violence is impossible. Through the power of voluntary suffering, the victims become no longer victims but instead active opponents in loving resistance to those who have refused to recognize them as human beings. The greater the repression, the greater must be the suffering courted by its victims; the greater the inhumanity, the greater the power of suffering love necessary to begin restoring the bonds of community. Suffering as such is powerless. Love transforms it into the kind of resistance capable of moving an opponent to acknowledge the victim's humanity.

We can understand, then, why Gandhi looked to Christ as the supreme example of nonviolence: on the cross suffering love received its fullest expression, even in the eyes of one who could not affirm Christ as uniquely divine. Gandhi knew that the man who died on Golgotha understood his entire life and mission as pointing toward that voluntary death, yet regarded it not as futility but as complete fulfillment. Jesus of Nazareth had no other purpose in life than the cross of suffering love, which is to say, he had no other purpose in life than life itself.

NONVIOLENCE AND REDEMPTION

But for the believer, the inner dynamic of redemption can also be understood in terms of nonviolence. If it is the purpose of nonviolence to move human beings by suffering love to a recognition of their common humanity, it is the purpose of the cross to move us in the same way to a recognition of all human beings in Christ. The cross moves us, first of all, to an acknowledgment of Jesus' own suffering humanity. In order to profess a faith in Christ, as Peter and the disciples learned, we must profess him first in the scandal of suffering and rejection which summarizes his humanity. But to identify oneself in faith with the Christ of the cross is to acknowledge that here is the ultimate self-disclosure of God in humanity, in the action of suffering love unto death and in the words of Christ embracing all men and women, victims and executioners alike: "Father, forgive them for they know not what they do." With these words and with the cross embodying them, Jesus revealed so profound a union between himself and humanity that the crucifixion cannot be seen in isolation from a single injustice in history, nor can it be separated from the personal confrontation of victim and executioner in any single injustice. By the crucifixion violence and injustice have everywhere become *crucial*, cross-centered.

In inflicting violence on one another, human beings know not what they do, for they know not the sacredness of their brothers' and sisters' and their own humanity, which at its innermost core is one with the humanity of Christ. The violence of human beings at any place or time in history is the violence of Golgotha. And the victim is everywhere and always the same: the man of the cross. To recognize the humanity of the Christ of the cross is to recognize all human beings in him, who in his suffering is one with all those by whom he has been murdered. To pass over to the suffering servanthood of the human Jesus is to see, through his forgiveness, his redeeming presence in all men and women, oppressed and oppressors alike, and to see therefore the possibility of his redeeming mediation of any human conflict through suffering love. To profess a living faith in the Christ of the cross is to affirm the redemptive reality present in every cross of suffering love enacted in history. Christ becomes present everywhere in suffering servanthood and crucifixion. In and through this presence he redeems humanity from division and leads it into community.

In thus interpreting the cross from the standpoint of belief, we may again confirm that interpretation best by returning to the witness of Gandhi. When India finally gained its independence from England in 1947, Gandhi could take no part in the victory celebrations. The partition of India and the creation of Pakistan had been accepted, against Gandhi's plea for unity, as the necessary condition for independence. The ensuing, intensified Hindu-Muslim conflict threatened to inflame both countries. Against the rise of mass violence, independence was an empty victory. Therefore, the 78-year-old Gandhi went to Calcutta, into a Muslim house in an area where the stones were slippery with fresh blood and the air acrid with the smoke of burning homes, and there he undertook a fast unto death. His fast would end only if and when sanity returned to Calcutta.

To most Indians, as to the other people of the world, Gandhi's decision to fast seemed irrelevant to the violent city about him. Yet Calcutta's response to Gandhi's self-imposed suffering grew as his suffering deepened and threatened to take his life. Even for the majority who could not understand Gandhi's methods or philosophy, it struck them that if anyone had to suffer for the continued killing of the city, it should not be Gandhi. Many wanted to stop his suffering. They gathered weapons from streets and homes and brought them to Gandhi offering them in return for his promise to break the fast. But Gandhi persisted, continuing his suffering until the city itself began to fast and suffer with him. Hindu and Muslim alike shared his pain and through that sharing the power of feeling was restored to a community which had become numbed to its inhumanity by constant violence.

As Dr. Amiya Chakravarty has written of the fast: "Suffering was happening in a social and moral vacuum, with no response from peoples whose minds had lost all human sensitiveness. It could only be reciprocated and then redeemed by the process of suffering. Then, out of sharing and involvement would arise a new situation; it would not be merely change but transformation."

When the fast was finally broken. Calcutta rejoiced and the warring communities joined in great feasts, while Gandhi sipped his glass of orange juice.

The transformation which Gandhi sought and was given through the cross is the transformation spoken of by the angel at the open tomb: "He is not here; for he has risen." Or more pointedly in Luke, "Why do you seek the living among the dead?" The cross raises the dead to the living because the cross itself is living, as Gandhi described and followed it. For Gandhi dared not think of birth without death on the cross. He also said, "God did not bear the cross only 1900 years ago, but He bears it today, and He dies and is resurrected from day to day." To the suffering servant, resurrection is as present a reality as crucifixion, although present only in and through the cross. Only in yielding up one's spirit, "Father, into thy hands I commit my spirit," is there granted the power to roll back the rock so that the dead can become the living. Only in suffering love unto death is a Calcutta reclaimed from the valley of the dead. Only through the servant's gift of life in the darkness of death can the violent be returned to life, for it was after Jesus' death that the centurion and those who assisted him in that death confessed, "Truly this was the Son of God."

Does not a full commitment to Jesus' humanity of suffering servanthood necessarily involve an existential commitment to the overcoming truth of his divinity as well? To answer yes with particular reference to Gandhi's witness is not to claim Gandhi for Christianity, but to claim to see the full meaning of Christ through Gandhi, in a living cross and resurrection which would be true to Gandhi's own understanding of what it means to live and to die. The cross is revolutionary not simply because it raises men and women to another life but because it transforms them into the fullness of that life on this earth. The revolution of peace is realized in Calcutta, not heaven, because only the wounded flesh and spilled blood of Calcutta can provide the matter of a new heaven and a new earth. The spirit of a new earth must also be in Calcutta, as it was in the Christic figure suffering into love the violence of the city, and in the community thus recreated.

Because he envisioned the face of God as Truth, Gandhi experimented with truth in a lifelong struggle to see God face to face. In the course of that struggle, which became in part the struggle of India and finally the British Empire and the world, Gandhi encountered God as suffering love. In realizing through his experiments that the God of Truth is found through the God of suffering love, Gandhi passed into the redeeming truth of the Incarnation.

Chapter Eight

The Mahatma and the Missioner

Bob McCahill, M.M.

Bob McCahill is a Maryknoll priest who has worked for sixteen years in Bangladesh.

One day, as I searched a dusty bookshelf for anything that could hold my interest, I happened upon a booklet by Mahatma Gandhi entitled "The Message of Jesus Christ." Reading it made my heart glow. In it, Gandhi more than confirmed my belief that for the people of Bangladesh, where I live, deeds of love and respectful presence among them are the most important gifts I have to offer. Gandhi convinced me that these God-fearing people love their own faiths as much as I love mine. His example showed me that an intelligent, courageous, and exceptionally open-minded person, who is also deeply knowledgeable about Jesus, Christianity, and Christians, can and should remain a part of the faith that nourishes him or her. Although Gandhi gave prolonged and prayerful consideration to becoming a Christian, Christianity simply did not compel his belief. Not from stubbornness, but from grace, I imagine, he renewed his devotion to the faith into which he was born. In that way, Gandhi reinforced my feelings of friendship for the faithful of other traditions and respect for the faiths they love. At the same time, Gandhi proposed for me an incarnated approach to these good people, by way of service and simplicity of life among them.

I had only recently come to Bangladesh after having spent eleven years as a missioner in the Philippines when I happened upon the booklet. In the Philippines, I had tried to witness to God's love for the poor by spending myself as a teacher and preacher, by giving spiritual seminars in the barrios of Mindanao, offering Masses, and administering sacraments among good people who practiced folk Catholicism. Now, in Bangladesh, I was searching for a new mode of witness. Gandhi's input was timely and pivotal for my understanding of the witness I am called to give among Muslims and Hindus

109

in Bangladesh. He assured me that among the people of Bangladesh the witness of good works and sacrifice for others that springs from the love of God would have an unrivalled impact upon the hearts of the persons served.

A DIALOGUE OF LIFE

Bangladesh has only been a nation since 1971. At that time, many Hindus evacuated to India, and many Muslims transferred from India to Bangladesh. At present, there are about 115 million people, 85% of whom are Muslims and 14% of whom are Hindus. It is a crowded place. The area is equivalent to the state of Iowa, but with forty times the population. Bangladesh is a rich deltic plain. Lush vegetation shoots up quickly from what some regard as the most fertile soil in the world. Most of the people are farm laborers, although the majority of them own no land. Natural disasters occur frequently: floods, tidal waves, cyclones, and tornados. The Bangladeshi people endure all these hardships and resume singing at the first appropriate opportunity. Music, poetry, and argument are favored sources of entertainment. They are a handsome, animated, eloquent, and curious people. Though only 23% of them are literate, oral traditions are stashed in their memories as wealth indestructible. Sufism has easily found a home in the Bengali temperament. While there are outstanding exceptions, most Muslims do not consider themselves to be especially pious. Nevertheless, they appreciate those Muslims who pray five times daily, and they admire Muslims who, even though materially as poor as themselves, offer alms to persons still less fortunate. They try to fulfill the yearly fast for as many of the thirty days as they can resist the pangs of hunger. Nevertheless, although they may be unable to perform all the practices of orthodox Islamic piety, the huge majority take great pride in being Muslim.

In general, the attitude toward Christian missioners on the part of both Muslims and Hindus is similar. That is, both are skeptical and suspicious. However, Hindus feel less threatened by missioners than do Muslims because their religion can absorb other points of view more easily. The expectation of both Muslims and Hindus is that missionaries come among them to snare converts. In view of that expectation, their tolerance for Christian missionaries is, on the whole, edifying.

Bangladeshis seldom ask me about my beliefs. Both Muslims and Hindus have strong, positive ideas about Jesus. They have learned of him and love him from their own Islamic and Hindu teachers. They think they know what Christians believe, so there is no need to inquire. What they do ask, insistently, is "Who are you?" and "What are you doing here?"

I explain: "I am your Brother Bob, a Catholic Christian missionary. I am here to serve seriously sick persons who are poor. Service to the needy and love for all persons is my purpose in life. Christians believe that Allah makes happy those who serve the needy." To some others, I say: "This Christian wishes you well. I appreciate your faith and your culture. There is nothing about you that I seek to change except that which you also wish changed," that is, ill health in exchange for good. To still others, I say: "I am your Christian brother. I am a missionary, that is, a servant of all God's people. Jesus went about doing good and healing because he loved God, and anyone who truly loves God also loves other people. I follow Jesus. I wish to help the widow, the orphan, and persons afflicted in any grievous way. Your religion and mine both teach that those who serve the poor serve Allah. I respect your Islamic faith. It is good. So is my Christian faith good. You fulfill your faith; I'll fulfill mine. We shall meet again in Paradise."

When it is the police who question me about my purpose for living in a town where there are no Christians, I hand them a copy of the letter of assignment given to me by Bishop Francis. He states five priorities: "Live among the poor as a brother to them. Serve the sick so that they may live. Show the respect which our Christian religion has for Islam and Hinduism. Explain to those who inquire about the reason for your lifestyle and good works. Contact the Christians in the area (a scattered few) and encourage them to live good lives."

In a crowded neighborhood named Islampur, I live in a hut made of bamboo, like the homes of my neighbors. In this 13 by 7 foot room, covered by a low tin roof, I pray, cook twice daily, rest, and store my bicycle. The hut has no electric current. Water is available only at a nearby tubewell, shared with many, as is the toilet. "Why don't you live in a house having an overhead fan?" sympathetic people ask me daily during the hottest months. They like to hear me repeat: "When you can do it then so will I." They appreciate that the bicycle is used for their benefit, and that it makes possible the seeking and finding of disabled persons in many distant villages and bazaars.

I draw encouragement from the Good News for this apostolate. Spend yourself (Matthew 20:28), serve others (John 13:15), go and heal (Acts 10:38), practice your religion openly (James 1:27), and expect rewards from God alone (Luke 14:14). I draw inspiration also from Gandhi's counsel, adapted to these people and to this time: "A life of service and uttermost simplicity is the best preaching."

DISINTERESTED SERVICE

The people of Bangladesh have a name for the sort of service that expects nothing in return. They call it disinterested. They believe it is either rare or nonexistent. Thus, they look for hidden, selfish motives in the good works of every missioner. They do not trust missioners. It is a lesson they learned from their colonial history. They perceive that missionaries speak of salvation while on their minds is the conquest of those who follow Islam or Hinduism. The missioner is after something: our conversion. Genuine altruism does not exist in the missioner's heart. He has an angle.

In one sense, missioners have been a stumbling block to mutual respect between Muslims, Hindus, and Christians. Some missioners have, indeed, offered service to the people for the purpose of bringing them into a church. Muslims and Hindus do not regard such service as noble, for it aims at procuring a reward, that is, the conversion of Muslims and Hindus to Christianity. Such efforts are regarded by them as no more worthy of admiration than the attempts of a salesperson to sell a product which no one wants. Bangladeshis have told me: "There are no disinterested persons." Gandhi observed that the use of education and health care as a means for attracting Muslims and Hindus to the Christian faith is proof for them that missionaries are as selfish and self-interested as anyone else.

It is the spirit of disinterested love, illustrated by acts of mercy on behalf of afflicted persons, which touches the hearts of the Muslims of Bangladesh. Their response to compassion convinces me that nothing affects them more deeply than this disinterested, and therefore, totally unexpected, concern shown by a Christian toward Muslims. Genuine altruism astounds them. "What you are doing for our people is very good!" they tell me. "Don't you know that people stay up nights talking about the fact that you wear sandals and not shoes, ride a push-bike and not an automobile?" As one laborer put it to his companions, dramatically: "This man practices Islam better than we do!" Positive feedback of this kind reaches me from time to time.

Missioners in Bangladesh serve the purpose of Christianity better by disinterested service to the poor than by proselytizing them. It was Gandhi's view, and it is mine. Our services are determined by the people's needs. The poor among whom I live feel the need for an intermediary when they are seriously ill. Without such a helper, oftentimes, they will not seek medical attention, even though government health institutions exist in virtually every locality to assist them. I invite the sick ones to those hospitals and clinics and introduce them to the doctors. The ailing ones regard my assistance as crucial. That no reward is solicited from them for helping them and accompanying them causes them to reconsider their idea of Christian missionaries. In addition to them, those who merely witness disinterested service as it is rendered to the poor, that is, other persons including the educated and those who are not poor, pause to reflect: Is it possible that the missioner treats my brother and sister Muslims as his own brothers and sisters without any intention to convert them? What new teaching is this?

A HARD LOOK AT CONVERSION

In this part of the world the need for tolerance and respect between religions is huge. Religiously inspired riots flared frequently in Gandhi's time; there is still fear of riots today. Gandhi believed that proselytization brought with it conflict. "The transference of allegiance from one fold to another and the mutual decrying of rival faiths gives rise to mutual hatred."

A question that Muslim men have put to me, as a test, is: "What will I receive if I become a Christian?" The majority of the inquirers are merely displaying their contempt for the alleged willingness of some missioners to tempt the poor and purchase their conversion. Although the missioners who strive to make converts are not principally Catholics, we Catholic missioners share their notorious reputation by association. Muslims' profoundly negative perception of all missioners will perdure for as long as some missioners continue to stress the conversion of Muslims as the goal of mission in Bangladesh.

Sixteen years of living closely with Muslims teaches me that they are quite suspicious that missioners do good to the poor solely in order to convert them to Christianity. Sad to say, there is some historical basis, in fact, for that perception. The most effective remedy for this jaundiced Muslim view is, in my experience, for the missioner to foreswear conversion as the purpose of mission.

There are persons who tell me in private that they are willing to become Christians if I will reciprocate with a loan, a scholarship, or a job. They would use their conversion as a commodity to be bartered for material benefits which I must provide. What does the Church tell me about dealing with such persons? The teaching is clear: "Material inducements carry a hint of coercion or a kind of persuasion that would be dishonorable or unworthy, especially when dealing with poor or uneducated people" (Declaration on Religious Freedom, Second Vatican Council). Where missioners are perceived to be sources of foreign largesse, as they are in Bangladesh, the temptation for some persons to convert in order to gain material advantages is great.

The intention to make converts from among other Christian denominations also needs to be excluded. In a village twenty miles away from me a community of Christians had lived united for half a century. A missioner from another denomination arrived and, finding himself unable to make converts from among the Muslims and Hindus in that locality, he turned his energies on the old Christians. Now, that village is divided between the two denominations. Their Muslim and Hindu neighbors ridicule the converters for having offered material inducements, and they poke fun at the converts who gave up their religion for a bribe. Peace is less in evidence now than before that preacher of the faith arrived. Christianity is derided in that locality.

FOLLOWING JESUS

It is not my purpose to preach Christian faith by word of mouth to Muslims and Hindus. I try, rather, to convey that faith through my behavior and works of compassion. Whenever they see attention and kindness bestowed on persons who are strangers to me, they ask me: "What gain is in it for you?" I reply: "Following Jesus' example gives my heart happiness. God's blessing is all the reward I want. My mother and father, sisters and brothers, are overjoyed that their son and brother spends his life in this way because their generosity will also be eternally rewarded by God." Muslims and Hindus are responding to the inspiration provided by God through their own religious faith. I respond to the inspiration given by God through Christian faith. We all intend and are striving to do the will of God, Allah, Bhagavan. They do the will of God in their way; I do it in my way. Oftentimes, our responses are alike. I do not judge their religions to be lacking. After all, they are frequently moved by their faiths to do those acts of virtue and good works which my religion urges me to do.

Gandhi counseled: "If you want us to feel the aroma of Christianity, you must copy the rose. The rose irresistibly draws people to itself, and the scent remains with them." At the outset of my stay in Bangladesh I paid a visit to an elderly missioner who had long years of experience working among Muslims. His story helped me to decide on the service I would offer to Muslims. This wise man had sought to convince and convert Muslims to Christianity during ten prime years of missionary endeavor. For, he explained, at that time, conversion was the focus of mission work. Try as he might, he was unable to convert a single Muslim to Christianity. Then one day, as he stood conversing with an educated young Muslim, they both observed a man sprawled in the gutter of the street. Two women wearing identical white garbs appeared, approached the man, went down to him and ministered to him. When next the missionary looked at this Muslim acquaintance's face, he was surprised to find him in tears. The sisters' active compassion had touched him. The young Muslim did not thereafter seek to become a Christian. Islam also stresses mercy and compassion toward the afflicted. However, he did understand compassion better, thanks to the example of two Catholic sisters. Their practical illustration of love, no doubt, remains with him until this day. Good example irresistibly draws all persons of good will, no matter what their religion is, and makes them more aware of the possibilities to do and to be good. Although this example occurred years after Gandhi's death, he would have understood perfectly the tearful appreciation of the Bengali Muslim. "Do not preach the God of history, but show Him as He lives today through you" — this was Gandhi's advice to missioners. The two sisters had uttered not a word about religion to the man in the gutter. Yet, they changed not only his life but also the lives of all who saw their love.

Bangladeshi Christians sometimes ask me: "What results do you have to show for years of living among Muslims?" I reply: "Nothing tangible," because there is no physical memorial of this work, e.g., no schools started, parishes established, or cooperatives begun. However, I do seem to have a lot of Muslim friends and well-wishers, most of whom were initially suspicious of "the missionary." Later, they came to be surprised by his love for the poor and respect for their faith. These Muslims have ended up speaking respectfully, and sometimes even enthusiastically, about the missioner's life and the service he gives without expectation of reward. Trust and friendship are growing.

"Missionaries have to alter their attitude," advised Gandhi:

Today they tell people there is no salvation for them except through the Bible and through Christianity. It is customary to decry other religions and to offer their own as the one that can bring deliverance. That attitude should be radically changed. Let them appear before the people as they are, and try to rejoice in seeing Hindus become better Hindus and Muslims better Muslims. Let them start work at the bottom. Let them enter into what is best in their life and offer nothing inconsistent with it. That will make their work far more efficacious, and what they will say and offer to the people appreciated without suspicion or hostility. In a word, let them go to the people not as patrons, but as one of them, not to oblige them, but to serve them and to work among them.

I have seen that Islam and Hinduism help these good people, give them guidance and comfort, and move them to practice virtue. This is not the place or time for Christians to press ahead with missionary themes from the past, e.g., Christianity is best, other religions and their rites are false or silly, conversion to Christianity is the only path to salvation. The Church encourages in Christians a new attitude toward other faiths, an attitude with which Gandhi would have been more comfortable and for which he is at least indirectly responsible.

We have this direction for our relationship with Muslims: "Although in the course of the centuries many quarrels and hostilities have arisen between Christians and Muslims, this most sacred Synod urges all to forget the past and to strive sincerely for mutual understanding. On behalf of all humankind, let Christians and Muslims make common cause of safeguarding and fostering social justice, moral values, peace, and freedom" (Declaration on the Relationship of the Church to Non-Christian Religions, Second Vatican Council). This, then, is a time in Bangladesh for openness toward Muslims, respect for their beliefs, recognition of the spiritual fruits their faith yields for them, and determined Christian initiatives that aim to put cooperation where competition has been.

MANY PATHS TO GOD

I have read the Qur'an and the Hadith of the Islamic faith and they have informed me. Even more enriching and broadening, however, have been personal contacts with Muslims and Hindus. In particular, conversations and friendship with Hajji Abdul Mannan during my first year in Bangladesh added credibility and warmth to my conviction that we are meant by God to be brothers and sisters to men and women of other faiths. Close range involvement with ordinary Muslims and Hindus helps me more than any other way to appreciate and respect other persons and their religions. I know that I have been enriched by close contact with them. They enable me to understand that persons holding to immensely diverse religions share deeply many identical values. Through contact, I perceive that faith in God, under the banner of whatever religion, results in lives that are praiseworthy. Moreover, few things in life could lead me more surely to God than the certain knowledge that persons who believe in teachings dissimilar to Christian teachings also love God and practice virtue.

When I see Muslims giving alms, enduring the fast, offering prayers faithfully, or behaving mercifully or generously, it has the same kind of effect on me as has the study of the solar system. That is, it expands my mind and heart. It gives evidence to me that there is more to other faiths than meets the eye. Just as the universe is boundless and still expanding, so is my admiration and appreciation for persons of every faith and for their faiths.

There is one God and there are many paths to God. With Gandhi, I believe that. All of the paths that lead to God are good. It is impossible to judge another's path because we are not on it. We see their paths in a distorted way, from afar, from outside their souls wherein faith abides. Yet, we do see that many persons on other paths live virtuously. My experience is that hospitality, mercy, generosity, and tolerance characterize the Muslims I know.

When I see goodness in the lives of others I affirm them in my heart. It seems fitting to me that a missioner, that is, a person whom Muslims regard as an official representative of the Christian faith, openly praises persons who act mercifully, pray, give alms, fast, and undertake the pilgrimage. How thoughtful it makes Muslims and Hindus when I praise their works. Their amazed reaction is: Can it truly be that a Christian missioner admires Muslims and Hindus?

Principal Matiur Rahman once told me: "Our religions have the potential to unite humankind. In fact, we use religion to keep ourselves apart." The inclination we have to always compare ourselves with others, combined with our ignorance of the inner lives of Muslims and Hindus, contributes to our false sense of superiority. We tend to be judgmental and to search for the things that separate us from other religions.

I thank God for Mahatma Gandhi. Gandhi demonstrated a life of dedication, concern for others, and daring in the cause of God, while professing a faith other than Christianity. He knew Christian teaching and regarded much of it as beautiful and true. He was close to numerous Christian missionaries and was invited by them to become a Christian. He refused these invitations because his own religion, Hinduism, satisfied his soul. He refused, also, because he saw little in the lives of Christians that could motivate him to request baptism. Gandhi was a seeker after truth, a man who was grateful to God for the compelling message of the Sermon on the

Mount. One of his great services to Christians is to suggest that we do mission wrongly, or more, that we even go about mission in an unchristian manner. Because his knowledge and appreciation of Christianity was deep his criticism of Christian mission methods deserves my attention. He claimed to know a mission approach which, if followed, would both benefit the people and advance the saving mission of Jesus. "A life of service and of uttermost simplicity is the best preaching." My experience during sixteen years of living among his people is that Gandhi knew what he was talking about.

By the fruits of his life and his love for Jesus, we know Gandhi to have been a follower of Jesus, although not exclusively of Jesus. Because of Gandhi, I know that a Christ-like spirit can exist in unbaptized persons. His life and example prepare me to expect that heroic evangelical virtue can be exercised by those who are not formally Christians. Because I expect to find abundant goodness and virtue among Muslims and Hindus, I do find it. If I did not expect to find virtue among them, I would probably miss it.

I look at the Mahatma and think: How beautiful it is to be broad-minded. To complain about the existence of other religions, or to view them as a threat to our Christian preeminence, reveals narrowness of vision — as if God cannot abide within people who, though aware of the teachings of Christianity, choose to be or to remain Muslim or Hindu. How alike were the spirits of Gandhi and Pope John XXIII, who counseled in his last testament: "Love one another. Seek rather what unites, not what may separate you from one another."

God is greater than our hearts (1 John 3:20).